50 South Korean Breakfast Recipes for Home

By: Kelly Johnson

Table of Contents

- Kimchi Fried Rice (Kimchi Bokkeumbap)
- Korean Pancakes (Jeon)
- Savory Korean Porridge (Juk)
- Rice Cake Soup (Tteokguk)
- Soybean Paste Soup (Doenjang Jjigae)
- Korean Egg Soup (Gyeran Jjim)
- Seaweed Soup (Miyeok Guk)
- Korean Breakfast Bibimbap
- Korean Style Omelet (Gyeran Mari)
- Spicy Tofu Soup (Sundubu Jjigae)
- Grilled Mackerel (Godeungeo Gui)
- Sweet Potato Porridge (Goguma Juk)
- Braised Fish (Jorim)
- Korean Scallion Pancakes (Pa Jeon)
- Spicy Korean Noodles (Jajangmyeon)
- Beef Soup (Yukgaejang)
- Kimchi Stew (Kimchi Jjigae)
- Korean Steamed Egg (Gyeran Jjim)
- Korean Meatballs (Tteokgalbi)
- Korean Style Grilled Cheese (Cheese Tteokbokki)
- Fried Tofu (Dubujjim)
- Korean Pancake with Seafood (Haemul Jeon)
- Rice and Kimchi Stir-Fry (Kimchi Bokkeumbap)
- Korean Breakfast Soup with Noodles (Guksoo)
- Korean Chicken Soup (Samgyetang)
- Pickled Radish (Kkakdugi)
- Korean Style Scrambled Eggs (Gyeran Bokkeum)
- Spicy Pork Belly (Jeyuk Bokkeum)
- Korean Rice Balls (Jumeokbap)
- Sesame Leaf Pancakes (Kkaennip Jeon)
- Korean BBQ Breakfast Bowl
- Sweet and Savory Soybean Soup (Doenjang Guk)
- Braised Chicken (Dakjjim)
- Korean Kimchi Omelette
- Red Bean Soup (Pat Juk)
- Stir-Fried Cabbage (Baechu Bokkeum)

- Korean Hotteok (Sweet Pancakes)
- Pork and Vegetable Soup (Dwaeji Guk)
- Spicy Rice Cake (Tteokbokki)
- Korean Egg Drop Soup (Gyeran Guk)
- Mung Bean Pancakes (Bindaetteok)
- Noodle Soup (Jajangmyeon)
- Grilled Vegetables (Yachae Gui)
- Korean BBQ Beef Skewers (Bulgogi)
- Spicy Fish Stew (Maeuntang)
- Korean Millet Porridge (Gyeolcheon Juk)
- Seafood Pancake (Haemul Pajeon)
- Kimchi and Pork Stir-Fry (Kimchi Jorim)
- Korean Tofu and Vegetable Stir-Fry (Dubujeongol)
- Traditional Korean Breakfast (Jangjorim with Rice)

Kimchi Fried Rice (Kimchi Bokkeumbap)

Ingredients:

- 2 cups cooked white rice (preferably cold or day-old)
- 1 cup kimchi, chopped
- 1/2 cup kimchi juice (optional, for extra flavor)
- 2 tablespoons vegetable oil
- 1 small onion, diced
- 2 cloves garlic, minced
- 1/2 cup diced carrots
- 1/2 cup diced bell peppers (any color)
- 2 green onions, chopped
- 2 large eggs
- 2 tablespoons soy sauce
- 1 tablespoon gochujang (Korean red chili paste), optional for extra heat
- 1 tablespoon sesame oil
- 1 tablespoon sesame seeds (for garnish)
- Fresh cilantro or green onions (for garnish, optional)

Instructions:

1. **Prepare Ingredients:**
   - Make sure your rice is cold and separated to avoid clumps.
   - Chop the kimchi and set aside.
2. **Cook the Vegetables:**
   - Heat vegetable oil in a large skillet or wok over medium-high heat.
   - Add the diced onion and cook until translucent, about 3 minutes.
   - Add the minced garlic and cook for an additional 1 minute until fragrant.
3. **Add Kimchi:**
   - Stir in the chopped kimchi and cook for 2-3 minutes, allowing it to heat through and release its flavor.
   - If using, add the kimchi juice and stir well.
4. **Add Vegetables:**
   - Add the diced carrots and bell peppers. Cook until the vegetables are tender, about 3-4 minutes.
5. **Add Rice:**
   - Add the cold rice to the skillet. Break up any clumps and stir everything together, allowing the rice to fry and pick up the flavors from the vegetables and kimchi.
6. **Season the Rice:**
   - Add soy sauce and gochujang (if using). Stir well to coat the rice evenly with the seasonings.
7. **Scramble Eggs:**

- Push the rice mixture to one side of the skillet. Crack the eggs into the empty space and scramble them until fully cooked.
   - Once cooked, mix the scrambled eggs into the rice.
8. **Finish:**
   - Drizzle sesame oil over the rice and mix well.
   - Stir in the chopped green onions.
9. **Garnish and Serve:**
   - Garnish with sesame seeds and additional green onions or cilantro, if desired.
   - Serve hot, either on its own or with additional kimchi on the side.

Enjoy your delicious Kimchi Fried Rice! It's a perfect, quick meal with a great balance of tangy, spicy, and savory flavors.

Korean Pancakes (Jeon)

Ingredients:

- **For Basic Jeon Batter:**
    - 1 cup all-purpose flour
    - 1 cup water (or cold water for a lighter batter)
    - 1 egg
    - 1/2 teaspoon salt
    - 1/4 teaspoon black pepper
- **For Vegetable Jeon:**
    - 1 cup shredded zucchini (excess moisture squeezed out)
    - 1 cup shredded carrots
    - 1 cup thinly sliced bell peppers
    - 1 cup thinly sliced onions
    - 1/2 cup chopped green onions
- **For Seafood Jeon (optional):**
    - 1/2 cup chopped shrimp or squid (optional)
- **For Cooking:**
    - 2-3 tablespoons vegetable oil
- **For Dipping Sauce:**
    - 3 tablespoons soy sauce
    - 1 tablespoon rice vinegar
    - 1 teaspoon sesame oil
    - 1 teaspoon sugar
    - 1 clove garlic, minced
    - 1 teaspoon sesame seeds
    - 1 tablespoon chopped green onions

Instructions:

1. **Prepare the Batter:**
    - In a large bowl, whisk together the flour, water, egg, salt, and pepper until smooth. Adjust the consistency with more water if needed; it should be pourable but not too runny.
2. **Prepare the Vegetables and Seafood:**
    - If making vegetable jeon, mix the shredded zucchini, carrots, bell peppers, onions, and green onions into the batter.
    - If making seafood jeon, add the chopped shrimp or squid to the batter as well.
3. **Cook the Jeon:**
    - Heat a non-stick skillet or frying pan over medium heat and add 1-2 tablespoons of vegetable oil.
    - Once the oil is hot, pour in a portion of the batter, spreading it out into a thin, even layer (about 1/4 inch thick).

- Cook until the edges start to crisp up and the bottom is golden brown, about 2-3 minutes. Flip and cook the other side until golden brown and crispy, another 2-3 minutes.
   - Remove from the pan and place on a plate lined with paper towels. Repeat with the remaining batter, adding more oil as needed.
4. **Make the Dipping Sauce:**
   - In a small bowl, combine the soy sauce, rice vinegar, sesame oil, sugar, minced garlic, sesame seeds, and chopped green onions. Stir until the sugar is dissolved.
5. **Serve:**
   - Cut the jeon into bite-sized pieces and serve warm with the dipping sauce.

Tips:

- **For a Crispier Texture:** Use cold water in the batter and cook on medium-high heat.
- **Variations:** You can add other ingredients like kimchi, mushrooms, or chives to the batter for different flavors.

Enjoy your Korean Pancakes (Jeon) as a tasty appetizer, side dish, or even a light main course!

Savory Korean Porridge (Juk)

Ingredients:

- **For Basic Juk:**
    - 1 cup short-grain or sushi rice (uncooked)
    - 6 cups water or low-sodium chicken broth
    - 1 tablespoon sesame oil
    - Salt, to taste
- **For Additional Flavors:**
    - 1 cup diced or shredded cooked chicken (optional)
    - 1/2 cup diced mushrooms (shiitake, button, or your choice)
    - 1/2 cup finely chopped spinach or bok choy
    - 1 small carrot, finely diced
    - 2 green onions, chopped
    - 2 cloves garlic, minced
- **For Garnish:**
    - 1 tablespoon sesame oil (for drizzling)
    - 1 tablespoon sesame seeds
    - 1-2 tablespoons chopped fresh cilantro or green onions
    - Pickled radish or kimchi (optional, for serving)

Instructions:

1. **Prepare the Rice:**
    - Rinse the rice under cold water until the water runs clear. Drain well.
2. **Cook the Rice:**
    - In a large pot, combine the rinsed rice and 6 cups of water or chicken broth. Bring to a boil over medium-high heat.
    - Reduce the heat to low and simmer, uncovered, for about 30-40 minutes, stirring occasionally. The rice should break down and become porridge-like, with the grains partially dissolved.
3. **Add Flavorings:**
    - In a separate pan, heat the sesame oil over medium heat. Add the minced garlic and cook until fragrant, about 1 minute.
    - Add the diced mushrooms, carrots, and chicken (if using). Sauté for about 3-4 minutes until the vegetables are tender and the chicken is heated through.
4. **Combine and Simmer:**
    - Stir the cooked vegetables and chicken mixture into the pot of rice porridge.
    - Add the chopped spinach or bok choy and continue to cook for another 5-7 minutes, allowing the flavors to meld and the porridge to thicken. Season with salt to taste.
5. **Garnish and Serve:**

- Ladle the porridge into bowls. Drizzle with additional sesame oil, and sprinkle with sesame seeds and chopped cilantro or green onions.
- Serve hot with pickled radish or kimchi on the side, if desired.

Tips:

- **Texture:** Adjust the consistency by adding more water or broth if the porridge is too thick.
- **Variation:** You can use different proteins or vegetables according to your preference, such as beef, tofu, or various leafy greens.

Enjoy your comforting Savory Korean Porridge (Juk)! It's perfect for a warming breakfast or a soothing meal any time of the day.

Rice Cake Soup (Tteokguk)

Ingredients:

- **For the Broth:**
    - 8 cups beef or anchovy broth (or water if you prefer a lighter version)
    - 1/2 lb (225g) beef brisket or ribeye (optional, for added flavor)
    - 3-4 dried anchovies (optional, for anchovy broth)
    - 1 small onion, peeled
    - 2-3 garlic cloves, peeled
    - 1 piece of kombu (dried kelp) (optional, for added umami)
- **For the Soup:**
    - 1 lb (450g) fresh rice cakes (tteok, preferably sliced or in thin oval shapes)
    - 1 tablespoon sesame oil
    - 2-3 green onions, chopped
    - 1-2 eggs, beaten
    - 1 tablespoon soy sauce (for seasoning)
    - 1 teaspoon salt (or to taste)
    - 1/2 teaspoon ground black pepper (or to taste)
- **For Garnish:**
    - 1 tablespoon toasted sesame seeds
    - 1 tablespoon chopped green onions
    - 1/4 cup thinly sliced beef (cooked, optional)
    - 1-2 sheets of dried seaweed (gim), cut into thin strips (optional)

Instructions:

1. **Prepare the Broth:**
    - **For Beef Broth:** In a large pot, add 8 cups of water and the beef brisket (or ribeye). Bring to a boil over high heat, then reduce the heat to low and simmer for 30-40 minutes. Skim off any foam or impurities that rise to the surface.
    - **For Anchovy Broth:** In another pot, add 8 cups of water, dried anchovies, onion, garlic, and kombu (if using). Bring to a boil, then reduce the heat and simmer for 10-15 minutes. Remove the anchovies and kombu before using the broth.
2. **Prepare the Rice Cakes:**
    - If using frozen rice cakes, soak them in warm water for about 30 minutes to soften. Drain and set aside.
    - If using fresh rice cakes, you can skip this step.
3. **Cook the Beef (if using):**
    - Remove the cooked beef from the broth, shred it into thin strips, and set aside. Discard any bones or excess fat.
4. **Assemble the Soup:**
    - In a large pot, heat the sesame oil over medium heat. Add the chopped green onions and cook until fragrant, about 1 minute.

- Add the soaked rice cakes to the pot and stir to coat them with the oil and green onions.
- Pour in the prepared broth (beef or anchovy) and bring to a boil. Reduce the heat and simmer for about 5-10 minutes, or until the rice cakes are tender.

5. **Add Eggs and Seasoning:**
    - Slowly drizzle the beaten eggs into the simmering soup while stirring gently to create egg ribbons.
    - Season the soup with soy sauce, salt, and black pepper. Adjust the seasoning to taste.
6. **Serve:**
    - Ladle the soup into bowls and garnish with toasted sesame seeds, chopped green onions, and cooked beef strips if using. Sprinkle with thinly sliced seaweed if desired.

Tips:

- **Broth Variations:** You can adjust the type of broth according to your preference. Beef broth adds richness, while anchovy broth provides a lighter and more subtle flavor.
- **Rice Cake Texture:** For a more authentic texture, use Korean rice cakes (tteok), which are typically found in Asian grocery stores.

Enjoy your comforting and delicious Rice Cake Soup (Tteokguk)! It's a traditional dish that symbolizes the beginning of a new year and is perfect for special occasions or a hearty meal.

Soybean Paste Soup (Doenjang Jjigae)

Ingredients:

- **For the Broth:**
    - 6 cups water or low-sodium chicken broth
    - 1-2 tablespoons doenjang (Korean soybean paste)
    - 1-2 tablespoons gochujang (Korean red chili paste), optional for heat
- **For the Soup:**
    - 1/2 lb (225g) beef (such as brisket or ribeye), thinly sliced (optional)
    - 1 tablespoon vegetable oil
    - 1 small onion, sliced
    - 2 cloves garlic, minced
    - 1 medium potato, peeled and cubed
    - 1 small zucchini, sliced
    - 1/2 cup mushrooms (shiitake, button, or your choice), sliced
    - 1 cup tofu, cubed
    - 1-2 green chilies, sliced (optional, for extra heat)
    - 1 tablespoon soy sauce
    - 1 tablespoon sesame oil
    - 1 teaspoon sugar (optional, to balance flavors)
- **For Garnish:**
    - 1 tablespoon chopped green onions
    - 1 tablespoon toasted sesame seeds

Instructions:

1. **Prepare the Broth:**
    - In a large pot, bring the water or chicken broth to a boil.
    - Stir in the doenjang (and gochujang if using) until well combined. Reduce the heat to medium.
2. **Cook the Beef (if using):**
    - In a separate pan, heat the vegetable oil over medium-high heat.
    - Add the sliced beef and cook until browned and cooked through, about 5-7 minutes. Remove from heat and set aside.
3. **Add Vegetables:**
    - To the simmering broth, add the sliced onion and minced garlic. Cook for about 2 minutes until fragrant.
    - Add the cubed potatoes and cook for about 5 minutes until they start to soften.
    - Stir in the zucchini, mushrooms, and green chilies (if using). Continue to simmer for another 5 minutes.
4. **Add Tofu and Seasoning:**
    - Gently add the cubed tofu to the pot.

- Stir in the soy sauce, sesame oil, and optional sugar. Continue to simmer for another 5 minutes, allowing the flavors to meld and the vegetables to become tender.
5. **Finish and Serve:**
    - Taste the soup and adjust the seasoning if needed. You can add a bit more doenjang or soy sauce to taste.
    - Ladle the soup into bowls and garnish with chopped green onions and toasted sesame seeds.

Tips:

- **Doenjang Variations:** Different brands of doenjang have varying intensities. Adjust the amount based on your taste preference.
- **Substitutes:** If you don't have doenjang, you can use miso paste as a substitute, though the flavor will be slightly different.
- **Vegetable Variations:** Feel free to add other vegetables like spinach, napa cabbage, or carrots.

Enjoy your hearty and flavorful Soybean Paste Soup (Doenjang Jjigae)! It's a perfect comfort food that's both nutritious and satisfying.

Korean Egg Soup (Gyeran Jjim)

Ingredients:

- **For the Egg Mixture:**
    - 4 large eggs
    - 1 cup chicken broth or water
    - 1 tablespoon soy sauce
    - 1/2 teaspoon sesame oil
    - 1/4 teaspoon salt (or to taste)
    - 1/4 teaspoon white pepper (or to taste)
- **For Garnish:**
    - 1-2 green onions, chopped
    - 1 tablespoon sesame seeds
    - Optional: thinly sliced mushrooms or vegetables (like carrots, bell peppers)

Instructions:

1. **Prepare the Egg Mixture:**
    - In a mixing bowl, whisk together the eggs until well beaten.
    - Add the chicken broth (or water), soy sauce, sesame oil, salt, and white pepper. Mix until fully combined.
2. **Prepare the Steaming Setup:**
    - If you have a Korean jjimjilbang (steamer) or a steamer basket, you can use that. Alternatively, you can use a heatproof bowl placed inside a larger pot with a lid.
    - If using a bowl inside a pot, place a small trivet or a heatproof plate inside the pot to elevate the bowl above the water level.
3. **Steam the Egg Soup:**
    - Pour the egg mixture into a heatproof bowl.
    - Bring a pot of water to a boil. Place the bowl with the egg mixture on the trivet or plate inside the pot.
    - Cover the pot with a lid and reduce the heat to low. Steam for about 15-20 minutes, or until the egg mixture is set and has a custard-like consistency. Avoid stirring during steaming.
4. **Add Optional Ingredients:**
    - If using additional ingredients like mushrooms or vegetables, you can add them to the egg mixture before steaming or gently fold them into the cooked soup after steaming.
5. **Garnish and Serve:**
    - Once the egg soup is set, carefully remove the bowl from the pot.
    - Garnish with chopped green onions and toasted sesame seeds.
    - Serve hot.

Tips:

- **Consistency:** For a smoother texture, make sure to strain the egg mixture through a fine sieve before steaming.
- **Steaming Method:** Steaming on low heat prevents the eggs from becoming rubbery or overcooked. Ensure the water is simmering, not boiling rapidly.
- **Serving:** Gyeran Jjim is often served as a side dish with rice and other Korean dishes. It's light but flavorful, making it a great addition to any meal.

Enjoy your Korean Egg Soup (Gyeran Jjim)! It's a simple yet delicious dish that's perfect for a comforting meal.

Seaweed Soup (Miyeok Guk)

Ingredients:

- **For the Soup:**
    - 1 cup dried seaweed (miyeok), soaked in water
    - 6 cups beef broth (or water for a lighter version)
    - 1/2 lb (225g) beef (brisket, ribeye, or stew meat), thinly sliced
    - 1 tablespoon sesame oil
    - 2 cloves garlic, minced
    - 2 tablespoons soy sauce
    - 1 tablespoon fish sauce (optional, for extra umami)
    - Salt and black pepper, to taste
- **For Garnish (Optional):**
    - 1 tablespoon toasted sesame seeds
    - 1-2 green onions, chopped

Instructions:

1. **Prepare the Seaweed:**
    - Soak the dried seaweed in a bowl of water for about 20-30 minutes, or until it becomes soft and plump. Drain and cut into bite-sized pieces.
2. **Prepare the Beef:**
    - In a large pot, heat the sesame oil over medium-high heat.
    - Add the thinly sliced beef and cook until it is browned and cooked through, about 3-4 minutes.
    - Add the minced garlic and cook for an additional 1 minute until fragrant.
3. **Make the Broth:**
    - Add the beef broth (or water) to the pot with the cooked beef. Bring to a boil, then reduce the heat to low and simmer for about 10 minutes to allow the flavors to meld.
4. **Add Seaweed and Season:**
    - Stir in the soaked and drained seaweed. Continue to simmer for an additional 10-15 minutes, or until the seaweed is tender.
    - Season with soy sauce and fish sauce (if using). Adjust the seasoning with salt and black pepper to taste.
5. **Finish and Serve:**
    - Garnish with toasted sesame seeds and chopped green onions if desired.
    - Serve hot, typically with a bowl of steamed rice.

Tips:

- **Seaweed Texture:** Ensure the seaweed is fully softened before adding it to the soup. If the seaweed is still tough, it may need more soaking or simmering time.

- **Broth Variations:** Beef broth gives a richer flavor, but you can use vegetable or chicken broth for a lighter version. You can also add a few drops of soy sauce for more depth.
- **Additions:** For extra flavor, you can add a small piece of kombu (dried kelp) to the broth while simmering.

Enjoy your Seaweed Soup (Miyeok Guk)! It's a nutritious and comforting dish that's both hearty and soothing.

Korean Breakfast Bibimbap

Ingredients:

- **For the Bibimbap:**
    - 2 cups cooked white rice (preferably warm)
    - 1 cup spinach, blanched and squeezed dry
    - 1 cup bean sprouts, blanched
    - 1 small carrot, julienned
    - 1 small zucchini, julienned
    - 1/2 cup mushrooms (shiitake, button, or your choice), sliced
    - 1 tablespoon vegetable oil (for stir-frying)
    - 1/2 lb (225g) ground beef (or other protein like chicken, tofu, or beef strips)
    - 2 cloves garlic, minced
    - 1 tablespoon soy sauce
    - 1 tablespoon sesame oil
    - 1 tablespoon gochujang (Korean red chili paste) or to taste
    - 2 large eggs
    - 1 tablespoon sesame seeds
    - 1-2 green onions, chopped
    - Optional: kimchi, for serving
- **For the Sesame Spinach:**
    - 1 tablespoon sesame oil
    - 1 tablespoon soy sauce
    - 1 teaspoon minced garlic
    - 1 teaspoon sesame seeds
- **For the Bean Sprouts:**
    - 1 tablespoon sesame oil
    - 1 tablespoon soy sauce
    - 1 teaspoon minced garlic
    - 1 teaspoon sesame seeds

Instructions:

1. **Prepare the Vegetables:**
    - **Spinach:** Toss the blanched spinach with sesame oil, soy sauce, minced garlic, and sesame seeds. Set aside.
    - **Bean Sprouts:** Toss the blanched bean sprouts with sesame oil, soy sauce, minced garlic, and sesame seeds. Set aside.
    - **Carrots and Zucchini:** Heat vegetable oil in a pan over medium heat. Stir-fry the julienned carrots and zucchini separately until tender, about 3-4 minutes each. Season lightly with salt and pepper if desired.
2. **Prepare the Meat:**

- Heat a skillet over medium-high heat and add the ground beef. Cook until browned and fully cooked.
- Add minced garlic, soy sauce, and sesame oil to the beef. Stir and cook for another 1-2 minutes to allow the flavors to meld. Set aside.
3. **Fry the Eggs:**
    - In a separate pan, heat a small amount of vegetable oil over medium heat.
    - Crack the eggs into the pan and cook until the whites are set and the yolks are still runny (or cooked to your liking). You can also cook the eggs sunny side up or over-easy.
4. **Assemble the Bibimbap:**
    - In serving bowls, place a portion of warm rice at the bottom.
    - Arrange the prepared vegetables and meat around the rice, creating a colorful arrangement.
    - Place a fried egg on top of each bowl.
    - Drizzle with gochujang (Korean red chili paste) according to taste.
5. **Garnish and Serve:**
    - Garnish with sesame seeds and chopped green onions.
    - Serve with kimchi on the side if desired.

Tips:

- **Rice:** Using warm rice helps the flavors meld better with the toppings.
- **Gochujang:** Adjust the amount based on your preferred spice level. You can also mix gochujang with a bit of sesame oil and sugar to balance the heat.
- **Vegetable Variations:** Feel free to add or substitute other vegetables such as bell peppers, mushrooms, or napa cabbage.

Enjoy your Korean Breakfast Bibimbap! It's a vibrant and customizable dish that's perfect for starting the day on a delicious note.

Korean Style Omelet (Gyeran Mari)

Ingredients:

- **For the Omelet:**
    - 6 large eggs
    - 1/4 cup milk (optional, for a fluffier texture)
    - 1/4 teaspoon salt (or to taste)
    - 1/4 teaspoon black pepper (or to taste)
    - 1 tablespoon vegetable oil
- **For the Filling:**
    - 1 small carrot, finely diced
    - 1/2 cup chopped spinach or green onions (or a mix)
    - 1/4 cup finely chopped onion
    - 1/4 cup finely chopped bell pepper (any color)
    - Optional: 1/4 cup diced ham or cooked chicken
- **For Garnish (Optional):**
    - 1 tablespoon chopped fresh herbs (like parsley or chives)
    - 1/2 teaspoon sesame seeds

Instructions:

1. **Prepare the Filling:**
    - Heat a small amount of vegetable oil in a pan over medium heat.
    - Sauté the diced carrot, chopped spinach or green onions, onion, bell pepper, and optional diced ham or chicken until the vegetables are tender and the mixture is cooked through. Allow it to cool slightly.
2. **Prepare the Egg Mixture:**
    - In a large bowl, whisk together the eggs, milk (if using), salt, and black pepper until well combined and slightly frothy.
3. **Cook the Omelet:**
    - Heat a non-stick skillet or omelet pan over medium-low heat. Add a small amount of vegetable oil and spread it evenly across the surface of the pan.
    - Pour a portion of the egg mixture into the pan, tilting the pan to spread it evenly into a thin layer. Cook until the edges start to set but the center is still slightly runny, about 1-2 minutes.
4. **Add the Filling:**
    - Sprinkle a portion of the vegetable filling evenly over one half of the omelet.
5. **Roll the Omelet:**
    - Using a spatula, carefully lift and fold the side of the omelet with the filling over the other side to create a roll. Continue to cook for another 1-2 minutes, until the omelet is fully cooked through.
6. **Finish and Serve:**
    - Slide the rolled omelet onto a cutting board and let it cool slightly.

- - Slice the omelet into bite-sized pieces or desired portions.
  - Garnish with chopped fresh herbs and sesame seeds if desired.

Tips:

- **Pan Size:** Use a small or medium-sized pan for better control over the thickness of the omelet. A larger pan may result in a thinner omelet that's harder to roll.
- **Rolling Technique:** If you find it difficult to roll the omelet, you can also fold it into thirds or quarters.
- **Variations:** Feel free to customize the filling with other ingredients such as mushrooms, zucchini, or cheese.

Enjoy your Korean Style Omelet (Gyeran Mari)! It's a delicious and versatile dish that's perfect for breakfast, lunch, or as a side dish in a Korean meal.

Spicy Tofu Soup (Sundubu Jjigae)

Ingredients:

- **For the Soup:**
    - 1 tablespoon vegetable oil
    - 1/2 lb (225g) pork (such as pork belly, shoulder, or ground pork), thinly sliced or ground
    - 1 small onion, sliced
    - 2 cloves garlic, minced
    - 1 small carrot, thinly sliced (optional)
    - 1/2 cup mushrooms (shiitake, button, or your choice), sliced
    - 1-2 tablespoons gochugaru (Korean red chili flakes) or to taste
    - 1 tablespoon gochujang (Korean red chili paste)
    - 4 cups beef or vegetable broth (or water)
    - 1 package (14 oz or 400g) soft tofu (sundubu), or silken tofu
    - 1 tablespoon soy sauce
    - 1 tablespoon fish sauce (optional, for extra umami)
    - 1 teaspoon sesame oil
    - 1-2 green onions, chopped
    - 1 egg (optional, for added richness)
- **For Garnish:**
    - 1 tablespoon chopped green onions
    - 1 tablespoon sesame seeds
    - 1 small sheet of dried seaweed (gim), cut into thin strips (optional)

Instructions:

1. **Prepare the Ingredients:**
    - Slice or chop the pork, onion, carrot (if using), and mushrooms. Drain and cut the soft tofu into chunks.
2. **Cook the Pork:**
    - Heat the vegetable oil in a large pot over medium-high heat.
    - Add the pork and cook until browned and cooked through, about 5-7 minutes.
    - Add the sliced onion and minced garlic. Cook until the onion is translucent, about 2 minutes.
    - Stir in the gochugaru (Korean red chili flakes) and gochujang (Korean red chili paste). Cook for another 1-2 minutes until fragrant.
3. **Add the Broth and Vegetables:**
    - Pour in the beef or vegetable broth (or water) and bring to a boil.
    - Reduce the heat to medium and add the sliced carrots (if using) and mushrooms. Simmer for about 5-7 minutes until the vegetables are tender.
4. **Add Tofu and Seasonings:**

- Gently add the soft tofu to the pot. Stir gently to avoid breaking up the tofu too much.
- Season with soy sauce and fish sauce (if using). Adjust the seasoning with additional salt or soy sauce if needed.
- Stir in the sesame oil and let the soup simmer for another 5 minutes to allow the flavors to meld.

5. **Add the Egg (Optional):**
    - If using, crack an egg into the center of the soup and let it cook until the white is set but the yolk is still runny, about 2 minutes. You can gently stir the egg into the soup or leave it whole.
6. **Garnish and Serve:**
    - Ladle the soup into bowls and garnish with chopped green onions, sesame seeds, and dried seaweed strips if desired.
    - Serve hot with a bowl of steamed rice.

Tips:

- **Tofu:** Soft tofu (sundubu) is key for the traditional texture. If you can't find it, silken tofu is a good substitute.
- **Spice Level:** Adjust the amount of gochugaru and gochujang based on your spice preference. You can also add more if you like it spicier.
- **Vegetables:** Feel free to add other vegetables like spinach, zucchini, or bell peppers according to your preference.

Enjoy your Spicy Tofu Soup (Sundubu Jjigae)! It's a deliciously warming and flavorful dish that's perfect for a cozy meal.

Grilled Mackerel (Godeungeo Gui)

Ingredients:

- **For the Grilled Mackerel:**
    - 2 whole mackerel (about 1 lb each), cleaned and gutted
    - 1 tablespoon soy sauce
    - 1 tablespoon sesame oil
    - 2 cloves garlic, minced
    - 1 tablespoon gochugaru (Korean red chili flakes) or to taste
    - 1 tablespoon rice wine or sake (optional, for added flavor)
    - 1 tablespoon sugar (optional, for a touch of sweetness)
    - 1 teaspoon ground black pepper
    - 1 tablespoon vegetable oil (for grilling)
- **For Garnish:**
    - 1 tablespoon sesame seeds
    - 1-2 green onions, chopped
    - Lemon wedges (optional, for serving)

Instructions:

1. **Prepare the Mackerel:**
    - Rinse the mackerel under cold water and pat dry with paper towels.
    - Score the skin lightly with a knife in a few places to help the seasoning penetrate and to prevent the fish from curling up while grilling.
2. **Make the Marinade:**
    - In a small bowl, mix together the soy sauce, sesame oil, minced garlic, gochugaru, rice wine (if using), sugar (if using), and ground black pepper.
3. **Marinate the Fish:**
    - Brush the mackerel inside and out with the marinade, ensuring that the fish is well coated. Let it marinate for about 15-30 minutes. If you have time, marinating for longer will enhance the flavor.
4. **Preheat the Grill:**
    - Preheat your grill to medium-high heat. If using a grill pan, heat it over medium-high heat and lightly brush with vegetable oil.
5. **Grill the Mackerel:**
    - Place the mackerel on the grill or grill pan. Cook for about 4-5 minutes per side, or until the skin is crispy and the fish is cooked through. The flesh should flake easily with a fork and have an internal temperature of 145°F (63°C).
6. **Garnish and Serve:**
    - Transfer the grilled mackerel to a serving platter. Sprinkle with sesame seeds and chopped green onions.
    - Serve with lemon wedges on the side, if desired, and accompany with Korean side dishes like kimchi, pickled radish, and steamed rice.

Tips:

- **Grilling:** If using a charcoal grill, ensure that the coals are evenly heated for a consistent cooking temperature. For gas grills, maintain a medium-high heat.
- **Flipping:** Be gentle when flipping the fish to avoid breaking the skin. Use a wide spatula to support the fish when turning.
- **Side Dishes:** Grilled mackerel pairs well with a variety of Korean side dishes and banchan. Consider adding a fresh salad or steamed vegetables to complete the meal.

Enjoy your Grilled Mackerel (Godeungeo Gui)! It's a flavorful and satisfying dish that showcases the natural taste of mackerel and is perfect for a casual meal or special occasion.

Sweet Potato Porridge (Goguma Juk)

Ingredients:

- **For the Porridge:**
    - 2 medium sweet potatoes (about 1 lb), peeled and cubed
    - 1/2 cup glutinous rice (also known as sweet rice), rinsed
    - 4 cups water or low-sodium chicken broth
    - 1/4 cup sugar (or to taste, can be adjusted or substituted with honey or maple syrup)
    - 1/4 teaspoon salt (or to taste)
    - 1/2 teaspoon vanilla extract (optional, for added flavor)
    - 1 tablespoon sesame oil (optional, for added richness)
- **For Garnish (Optional):**
    - 1 tablespoon toasted sesame seeds
    - 1-2 tablespoons chopped nuts (such as walnuts or almonds)
    - 1-2 tablespoons dried fruit (such as raisins or goji berries)
    - Fresh fruit slices (such as apples or pears)

Instructions:

1. **Prepare the Sweet Potatoes:**
    - Peel and cube the sweet potatoes into small pieces. This helps them cook faster and blend smoothly.
2. **Cook the Sweet Potatoes:**
    - In a large pot, add the cubed sweet potatoes and water or chicken broth.
    - Bring to a boil over medium-high heat, then reduce the heat to low and simmer for about 10-15 minutes, or until the sweet potatoes are tender and easily mashable.
3. **Prepare the Rice:**
    - While the sweet potatoes are cooking, rinse the glutinous rice under cold water until the water runs clear.
4. **Blend the Mixture:**
    - Once the sweet potatoes are tender, use a potato masher or immersion blender to mash or blend them in the pot until smooth. If you don't have an immersion blender, you can transfer the sweet potatoes and some of the liquid to a regular blender and blend until smooth, then return it to the pot.
5. **Add the Rice:**
    - Stir the rinsed glutinous rice into the sweet potato mixture. Continue to cook over low heat, stirring occasionally, for about 20-30 minutes, or until the rice is fully cooked and the porridge has thickened to your desired consistency.
6. **Season the Porridge:**
    - Stir in the sugar, salt, and vanilla extract (if using). Adjust the sweetness to your taste. If you're using sesame oil, stir it in now for added richness.

7. **Serve and Garnish:**
   - Ladle the porridge into bowls and garnish with toasted sesame seeds, chopped nuts, dried fruit, and fresh fruit slices if desired.

Tips:

- **Texture:** If you prefer a smoother porridge, blend the mixture until completely smooth. For a more textured porridge, mash the sweet potatoes and leave some chunks.
- **Sweetness:** Adjust the sweetness to your preference. You can use less sugar or substitute with natural sweeteners like honey or maple syrup.
- **Consistency:** If the porridge is too thick, you can thin it with a little more water or broth until you reach your desired consistency.

Enjoy your Sweet Potato Porridge (Goguma Juk)! It's a warm and soothing dish that's perfect for a comforting meal.

Braised Fish (Jorim)

Ingredients:

- **For the Braised Fish:**
    - 2 whole fish (such as mackerel, cod, or bass), cleaned and gutted (about 1-1.5 lbs total)
    - 1 tablespoon vegetable oil
    - 1 small onion, sliced
    - 2 cloves garlic, minced
    - 1 small carrot, sliced
    - 1/2 cup daikon radish, sliced
    - 2-3 green chilies, sliced (optional, for heat)
    - 1 cup water or fish stock
- **For the Braising Sauce:**
    - 1/4 cup soy sauce
    - 2 tablespoons gochujang (Korean red chili paste) or to taste
    - 2 tablespoons brown sugar or honey
    - 1 tablespoon rice wine or sake (optional, for extra depth)
    - 1 tablespoon sesame oil
    - 1 teaspoon grated ginger
    - 1 teaspoon gochugaru (Korean red chili flakes) or to taste
    - 1/2 teaspoon black pepper
- **For Garnish (Optional):**
    - 1 tablespoon toasted sesame seeds
    - 1-2 green onions, chopped
    - Fresh cilantro or parsley (optional)

Instructions:

1. **Prepare the Fish:**
    - Rinse the fish under cold water and pat dry with paper towels. If the fish is not already pre-cut, you can cut it into fillets or leave it whole depending on your preference.
2. **Make the Braising Sauce:**
    - In a bowl, mix together the soy sauce, gochujang, brown sugar or honey, rice wine (if using), sesame oil, grated ginger, gochugaru, and black pepper.
3. **Sear the Fish:**
    - Heat the vegetable oil in a large pan or skillet over medium-high heat.
    - Add the fish to the pan and sear for 2-3 minutes on each side until lightly browned. This step adds depth of flavor and helps the fish hold together during braising.
4. **Add Vegetables and Sauce:**

- Remove the fish from the pan and set aside. In the same pan, add the sliced onion, minced garlic, sliced carrot, and daikon radish. Stir-fry for about 2 minutes until the vegetables start to soften.
- Return the fish to the pan and pour the braising sauce over the top.
- Add 1 cup of water or fish stock to the pan.

5. **Braise the Fish:**
   - Bring the liquid to a simmer. Reduce the heat to low, cover the pan, and let the fish braise for about 20-30 minutes, or until the fish is cooked through and the vegetables are tender.
   - Occasionally spoon some of the sauce over the fish to ensure it is well-coated.

6. **Finish and Serve:**
   - Once the fish is fully cooked, remove it from the pan and place it on a serving platter.
   - Increase the heat to medium-high and reduce the sauce if desired until it thickens slightly.
   - Pour the reduced sauce and vegetables over the fish.
   - Garnish with toasted sesame seeds, chopped green onions, and fresh herbs if desired.

Tips:

- **Fish Choice:** Mackerel is a popular choice for this dish due to its rich flavor, but you can use other firm fish like cod or bass.
- **Sauce Adjustment:** Adjust the sweetness or spiciness of the sauce according to your taste preference.
- **Vegetables:** Feel free to add or substitute other vegetables like bell peppers, mushrooms, or bok choy.

Enjoy your Braised Fish (Jorim)! It's a hearty and flavorful dish that pairs wonderfully with steamed rice and other Korean side dishes.

Korean Scallion Pancakes (Pa Jeon)

Ingredients:

- **For the Pancake Batter:**
    - 1 cup all-purpose flour
    - 1 cup cold water
    - 1/4 teaspoon salt
    - 1/4 teaspoon ground black pepper
    - 1/4 teaspoon sugar
    - 1 large egg
    - 1 cup chopped scallions (green onions)
    - 1/2 cup grated carrot (optional)
    - 1/2 cup chopped vegetables (e.g., bell pepper, mushrooms, optional)
    - 1/2 cup cooked meat (e.g., shrimp, pork, or beef, optional)
- **For Frying:**
    - 2-3 tablespoons vegetable oil
- **For the Dipping Sauce:**
    - 2 tablespoons soy sauce
    - 1 tablespoon rice vinegar
    - 1 teaspoon sesame oil
    - 1 teaspoon sugar
    - 1 clove garlic, minced
    - 1 teaspoon sesame seeds
    - 1-2 green onions, chopped
    - 1/2 teaspoon gochugaru (Korean red chili flakes) or red pepper flakes (optional, for heat)

Instructions:

1. **Prepare the Pancake Batter:**
    - In a large bowl, whisk together the flour, cold water, salt, black pepper, sugar, and egg until smooth.
    - Stir in the chopped scallions. If using, add the grated carrot, other vegetables, and cooked meat. Mix until everything is evenly distributed.
2. **Heat the Pan:**
    - Heat a non-stick skillet or frying pan over medium-high heat.
    - Add 1 tablespoon of vegetable oil and swirl to coat the bottom of the pan.
3. **Cook the Pancake:**
    - Pour about 1/4 to 1/3 cup of the batter into the hot pan and spread it out into a thin, even layer. You can make smaller pancakes for easier flipping or larger ones for a more substantial dish.
    - Cook for about 2-3 minutes, or until the edges start to turn golden brown and crispy.

- Flip the pancake carefully and cook the other side for an additional 2-3 minutes, or until golden brown and crispy.

4. **Repeat:**
   - Add more oil to the pan as needed and repeat the process with the remaining batter, making sure not to overcrowd the pan.
5. **Prepare the Dipping Sauce:**
   - In a small bowl, combine soy sauce, rice vinegar, sesame oil, sugar, minced garlic, sesame seeds, chopped green onions, and gochugaru (if using).
   - Stir until the sugar is dissolved and the ingredients are well mixed.
6. **Serve:**
   - Transfer the cooked pancakes to a plate and cut into wedges or bite-sized pieces.
   - Serve hot with the dipping sauce on the side.

Tips:

- **Consistency:** The batter should be slightly thick but pourable. Adjust the amount of water or flour as needed to achieve the right consistency.
- **Texture:** For extra crispiness, you can add a bit more oil to the pan while cooking.
- **Variety:** Feel free to customize the pancake by adding different vegetables or proteins according to your preference.

Enjoy your Korean Scallion Pancakes (Pa Jeon)! They're perfect for sharing with family and friends or as a delicious treat for yourself.

Spicy Korean Noodles (Jajangmyeon)

Ingredients:

- **For the Sauce:**
    - 3 tablespoons black bean paste (chunjang)
    - 2 tablespoons gochujang (Korean red chili paste)
    - 1 tablespoon soy sauce
    - 1 tablespoon sugar
    - 1 tablespoon rice wine or sake (optional, for depth of flavor)
    - 1/2 cup chicken or vegetable broth
    - 1 tablespoon sesame oil
- **For the Noodles and Stir-Fry:**
    - 8 oz (225g) fresh or dried jajangmyeon noodles (or substitute with udon or Chinese egg noodles)
    - 1 tablespoon vegetable oil
    - 1/2 lb (225g) pork belly or ground pork, cut into small pieces
    - 1 small onion, diced
    - 1 small zucchini, diced
    - 1/2 cup mushrooms (shiitake or button), sliced
    - 1/2 cup cabbage, shredded
    - 2 cloves garlic, minced
    - 1-inch piece of ginger, minced
    - 1-2 green chilies, sliced (optional, for extra heat)
- **For Garnish:**
    - 1 tablespoon sesame seeds
    - 2-3 green onions, chopped
    - 1/2 cucumber, julienned (optional, for freshness)
    - Pickled radish (kimchi or danmuji), for serving

Instructions:

1. **Prepare the Noodles:**
    - Cook the jajangmyeon noodles according to the package instructions. Drain and set aside.
2. **Make the Sauce:**
    - In a small bowl, mix together the black bean paste (chunjang), gochujang, soy sauce, sugar, rice wine (if using), chicken or vegetable broth, and sesame oil. Set aside.
3. **Stir-Fry the Ingredients:**
    - Heat vegetable oil in a large skillet or wok over medium-high heat.
    - Add the pork and cook until browned and cooked through, about 5-7 minutes.
    - Add the diced onion, zucchini, mushrooms, and cabbage. Stir-fry for another 3-4 minutes until the vegetables are tender.

- Add the minced garlic, ginger, and green chilies (if using). Stir-fry for 1-2 minutes until fragrant.
4. **Add the Sauce:**
    - Pour the prepared sauce over the pork and vegetable mixture. Stir well to combine and cook for another 2-3 minutes, allowing the sauce to thicken slightly.
5. **Combine with Noodles:**
    - Add the cooked noodles to the pan and toss gently to coat the noodles with the sauce and evenly distribute the ingredients. Cook for another 2-3 minutes until everything is heated through and well combined.
6. **Serve:**
    - Transfer the spicy jajangmyeon to serving plates.
    - Garnish with sesame seeds, chopped green onions, and julienned cucumber (if using).
    - Serve with pickled radish (kimchi or danmuji) on the side.

Tips:

- **Noodles:** If you're using dried noodles, cook them just until they're al dente, as they will continue to cook slightly when combined with the sauce.
- **Sauce:** Adjust the level of spiciness by modifying the amount of gochujang and green chilies.
- **Texture:** For extra texture, consider adding some crunchy vegetables or even tofu to the stir-fry.

Enjoy your Spicy Korean Noodles (Jajangmyeon)! This dish combines the rich flavors of the traditional jajangmyeon with a spicy kick for an exciting twist.

Beef Soup (Yukgaejang)

Ingredients:

- **For the Soup:**
    - 1 lb (450g) beef brisket or shank
    - 8 cups water
    - 1 onion, quartered
    - 4 cloves garlic
    - 1 piece of ginger (1-inch), sliced
    - 2 tablespoons soy sauce
    - 1 tablespoon sesame oil
    - 2 tablespoons gochugaru (Korean red chili flakes)
    - 1 tablespoon gochujang (Korean red chili paste)
    - 1 tablespoon soy sauce
    - 1 teaspoon sugar
    - 1 teaspoon black pepper
    - 1-2 green chilies, sliced (optional, for extra heat)
- **For the Vegetables and Garnish:**
    - 1 cup bean sprouts
    - 1 cup fernbrake (gosari) or dried bracken, soaked and cut into bite-sized pieces
    - 1 cup shredded napa cabbage
    - 1 small onion, thinly sliced
    - 1-2 green onions, chopped
    - 1 tablespoon sesame seeds (for garnish)

Instructions:

1. **Prepare the Beef:**
    - In a large pot, bring 8 cups of water to a boil. Add the beef brisket or shank, quartered onion, garlic cloves, and ginger slices.
    - Reduce the heat to low and simmer for 1.5-2 hours, or until the beef is tender and fully cooked. Skim off any foam that rises to the surface.
2. **Shred the Beef:**
    - Remove the beef from the pot and let it cool slightly. Discard the onion, garlic, and ginger.
    - Shred the beef into thin strips, removing any excess fat or connective tissue.
3. **Prepare the Soup Base:**
    - Return the shredded beef to the pot. Add soy sauce, sesame oil, gochugaru, gochujang, soy sauce, sugar, and black pepper. Stir well to combine.
4. **Add Vegetables:**
    - Add the bean sprouts, fernbrake (gosari), shredded napa cabbage, and thinly sliced onion to the pot.

- Simmer for an additional 10-15 minutes, or until the vegetables are tender and flavors are well combined.
5. **Finish and Serve:**
    - Taste and adjust seasoning as needed. You can add more soy sauce, gochugaru, or salt according to your preference.
    - Serve the soup hot, garnished with chopped green onions and sesame seeds.

Tips:

- **Fernbrake (Gosari):** If you can't find fernbrake, you can substitute with other vegetables like mushrooms or spinach. Fernbrake adds a unique texture and flavor to the soup.
- **Spice Level:** Adjust the amount of gochugaru and green chilies based on your heat preference.
- **Broth:** For a richer broth, you can simmer the beef bones along with the meat, or use beef stock instead of water.

Enjoy your Yukgaejang! This flavorful and spicy beef soup is perfect for warming up on a cold day or for a comforting meal any time.

Kimchi Stew (Kimchi Jjigae)

Ingredients:

- **For the Stew:**
    - 2 cups well-fermented kimchi, chopped (with some kimchi juice)
    - 1/2 lb (225g) pork belly or shoulder, cut into bite-sized pieces
    - 1 tablespoon vegetable oil
    - 1 small onion, sliced
    - 2 cloves garlic, minced
    - 1 tablespoon gochugaru (Korean red chili flakes)
    - 1 tablespoon gochujang (Korean red chili paste)
    - 4 cups water or chicken broth
    - 1 tablespoon soy sauce
    - 1 tablespoon sesame oil
    - 1 teaspoon sugar (optional, to balance the flavors)
    - 1 cup tofu, cut into cubes
    - 1 green onion, chopped (for garnish)
    - 1/2 teaspoon sesame seeds (for garnish)
- **Optional Ingredients:**
    - 1 small zucchini, sliced
    - 1 cup mushrooms (shiitake, button, or your choice), sliced
    - 1 small potato, peeled and diced
    - 1-2 green chilies, sliced (for extra heat)

Instructions:

1. **Prepare the Ingredients:**
    - Chop the kimchi and set aside. Cut the pork into bite-sized pieces. Slice the onion, mince the garlic, and prepare any additional vegetables you're using.
2. **Cook the Pork:**
    - Heat the vegetable oil in a large pot over medium-high heat.
    - Add the pork pieces and cook until they start to brown and release their fat, about 5-7 minutes.
3. **Add Aromatics and Kimchi:**
    - Add the sliced onion and minced garlic to the pot with the pork. Cook until the onion is translucent and fragrant, about 2 minutes.
    - Stir in the gochugaru and gochujang. Cook for another minute until the spices become fragrant.
4. **Add Kimchi and Liquid:**
    - Add the chopped kimchi (and some of the kimchi juice) to the pot. Stir well to combine.
    - Pour in the water or chicken broth and bring the mixture to a boil.
5. **Simmer the Stew:**

- Reduce the heat to medium-low and simmer for about 15-20 minutes, allowing the flavors to meld together. If you're adding additional vegetables like potatoes, zucchini, or mushrooms, add them at this stage.
6. **Add Tofu and Final Seasoning:**
    - Gently add the cubed tofu to the pot and stir carefully to avoid breaking the tofu. Simmer for another 5-10 minutes.
    - Season with soy sauce, sesame oil, and sugar (if using). Taste and adjust the seasoning as needed.
7. **Garnish and Serve:**
    - Ladle the stew into bowls. Garnish with chopped green onions and sesame seeds.
    - Serve hot with a bowl of steamed rice on the side.

Tips:

- **Kimchi:** Well-fermented kimchi works best for this stew as it adds a rich, tangy flavor. Adjust the amount based on your preference for spiciness and tanginess.
- **Pork:** If you prefer a leaner option, you can use chicken or omit the meat entirely for a vegetarian version.
- **Texture:** For a heartier stew, you can add more vegetables or use thicker slices of kimchi.

Enjoy your Kimchi Jjigae! It's a flavorful, satisfying stew that's perfect for warming up on a chilly day or anytime you crave a comforting Korean dish.

Korean Steamed Egg (Gyeran Jjim)

Ingredients:

- **For the Steamed Egg:**
    - 4 large eggs
    - 1 cup water or chicken broth
    - 1 tablespoon soy sauce
    - 1/2 teaspoon sesame oil
    - 1/4 teaspoon salt (or to taste)
    - 1/4 teaspoon black pepper
    - 1/4 teaspoon sugar (optional, for a touch of sweetness)
    - 2 green onions, finely chopped
    - 1/2 cup finely chopped vegetables (e.g., carrots, bell peppers, or mushrooms, optional)
    - 1/2 teaspoon sesame seeds (for garnish, optional)

Instructions:

1. **Prepare the Egg Mixture:**
    - Crack the eggs into a bowl and beat them lightly with a fork or whisk.
    - Add the water or chicken broth, soy sauce, sesame oil, salt, black pepper, and sugar (if using). Whisk until well combined.
2. **Add Vegetables (Optional):**
    - If using vegetables, finely chop them and mix them into the egg mixture.
3. **Prepare for Steaming:**
    - If you're using a traditional Korean earthenware pot (ttukbaegi), lightly grease the pot with a little oil or non-stick spray. Pour the egg mixture into the pot.
    - If you're using a heatproof bowl or a ramekin, you can grease it lightly as well before pouring in the egg mixture.
4. **Steam the Eggs:**
    - **Traditional Steaming Method:**
        - Bring a pot of water to a boil and place a steamer rack or a heatproof plate in the pot. The water level should be below the steamer rack.
        - Place the pot with the egg mixture on the rack. Cover with a lid and steam over medium-low heat for about 15-20 minutes, or until the eggs are set and puffed.
    - **Microwave Method:**
        - Cover the bowl or ramekin with microwave-safe plastic wrap or a microwave-safe lid.
        - Microwave on medium power (50%) for 4-6 minutes, checking every 1-2 minutes, until the eggs are fully set and have a fluffy texture.
5. **Garnish and Serve:**
    - Once the egg mixture is set, remove it from the steamer or microwave.

- Garnish with finely chopped green onions and sesame seeds if desired.

Tips:

- **Consistency:** The texture should be light and fluffy. Overcooking can lead to a dry texture, so keep an eye on it while steaming.
- **Flavor Variations:** You can add various seasonings or ingredients such as diced ham, cheese, or seafood to customize the flavor.
- **Serving:** Gyeran Jjim is best served immediately while it's warm and fluffy.

Enjoy your Gyeran Jjim! This classic Korean dish makes a great side for any Korean meal and is simple to prepare.

Korean Meatballs (Tteokgalbi)

Ingredients:

- **For the Meatballs:**
    - 1 lb (450g) ground beef (preferably a mix of beef and pork for more flavor and moisture)
    - 1/4 cup grated or finely chopped onion
    - 1/4 cup grated or finely chopped pear or apple (for sweetness and tenderness)
    - 2 cloves garlic, minced
    - 1 tablespoon ginger, minced
    - 2 tablespoons soy sauce
    - 1 tablespoon sesame oil
    - 1 tablespoon brown sugar or honey
    - 1/4 teaspoon black pepper
    - 1/2 teaspoon salt (adjust to taste)
    - 1 egg, lightly beaten
    - 1/4 cup breadcrumbs (optional, for texture)
- **For Garnish (Optional):**
    - 1 tablespoon toasted sesame seeds
    - 2-3 green onions, chopped

Instructions:

1. **Prepare the Ingredients:**
    - In a large bowl, combine the ground beef, grated onion, grated pear or apple, minced garlic, and minced ginger.
2. **Mix the Seasonings:**
    - Add the soy sauce, sesame oil, brown sugar or honey, black pepper, salt, and beaten egg to the meat mixture. If using, add the breadcrumbs to help bind the mixture and provide texture.
3. **Mix and Shape:**
    - Mix all the ingredients thoroughly until well combined. The mixture should be moist but not too sticky. If the mixture feels too wet, you can add a little more breadcrumbs.
    - Shape the mixture into small meatballs or patties, about 1-2 inches in diameter. You can also shape them into flat oval patties if you prefer.
4. **Cook the Meatballs:**
    - **Pan-Frying Method:**
        - Heat a little vegetable oil in a large skillet over medium heat.
        - Add the meatballs or patties to the pan and cook for about 3-4 minutes on each side, or until they are nicely browned and cooked through. You may need to cook them in batches to avoid overcrowding the pan.
    - **Grilling Method:**

- Preheat your grill to medium-high heat.
- Grill the meatballs or patties for about 3-4 minutes on each side, or until cooked through and slightly charred.

5. **Garnish and Serve:**
    - Transfer the cooked meatballs to a serving platter.
    - Garnish with toasted sesame seeds and chopped green onions if desired.
    - Serve hot with steamed rice and your favorite Korean side dishes.

Tips:

- **Texture:** The addition of grated pear or apple helps tenderize the meat and adds a subtle sweetness. You can use a food processor to finely grate the pear or apple.
- **Binding:** Breadcrumbs are optional but help with binding the mixture. If you want to avoid them, ensure the egg is well-mixed and the meat is not too wet.
- **Cooking:** Make sure the meatballs are cooked through and have an internal temperature of 160°F (71°C) to ensure they are safe to eat.

Enjoy your Tteokgalbi! These Korean meatballs are perfect for a flavorful meal and pair wonderfully with a variety of Korean dishes.

Korean Style Grilled Cheese (Cheese Tteokbokki)

Ingredients:

- **For the Tteokbokki:**
    - 1 lb (450g) Korean rice cakes (tteokbokki tteok), sliced into bite-sized pieces
    - 2 cups water
    - 1 cup Korean fish cake (eomuk), cut into bite-sized pieces (optional)
    - 2-3 tablespoons gochujang (Korean red chili paste)
    - 1 tablespoon gochugaru (Korean red chili flakes) (optional, for extra heat)
    - 2 tablespoons soy sauce
    - 1 tablespoon sugar or honey
    - 1 tablespoon minced garlic
    - 1 tablespoon sesame oil
    - 1/2 cup grated mozzarella cheese
    - 1/4 cup grated cheddar cheese (optional, for extra flavor)
    - 1 green onion, chopped (for garnish)
    - Sesame seeds (for garnish)
- **For Optional Toppings:**
    - 1/2 cup sliced mushrooms
    - 1/2 cup chopped vegetables (e.g., bell peppers, carrots)
    - 1 egg, boiled or poached (optional, for added richness)

Instructions:

1. **Prepare the Tteokbokki:**
    - If the rice cakes are refrigerated or frozen, soak them in warm water for about 10-15 minutes to soften. Drain and set aside.
    - In a large pan or skillet, add the water and bring to a simmer over medium heat.
2. **Make the Sauce:**
    - Stir in the gochujang, gochugaru (if using), soy sauce, sugar or honey, minced garlic, and sesame oil. Mix until well combined and the sauce is smooth.
3. **Cook the Tteokbokki:**
    - Add the rice cakes and fish cake (if using) to the pan. Stir to coat the rice cakes with the sauce.
    - Simmer for about 10-15 minutes, or until the rice cakes are heated through and the sauce has thickened. Stir occasionally to prevent sticking.
4. **Add Cheese:**
    - Once the tteokbokki is cooked and the sauce is thick, sprinkle the grated mozzarella cheese (and cheddar cheese, if using) over the top.
    - Cover the pan with a lid and let it cook for another 2-3 minutes, or until the cheese has melted and is bubbly.
5. **Serve and Garnish:**
    - Garnish with chopped green onions and sesame seeds.

- If using optional toppings, add the sliced mushrooms, chopped vegetables, or a boiled or poached egg at this stage.
6. **Optional – Broil for Extra Melty Cheese:**
   - For an extra cheesy finish, you can transfer the tteokbokki to an oven-safe dish, top with additional cheese, and place it under a broiler for 2-3 minutes until the cheese is bubbly and golden.

Tips:

- **Rice Cakes:** If you can't find Korean rice cakes, you can substitute with thick pasta or gnocchi, though the texture will be different.
- **Cheese:** Adjust the amount and type of cheese according to your preference. Mozzarella gives a classic gooey texture, while cheddar adds a sharper flavor.
- **Heat Level:** Adjust the amount of gochujang and gochugaru based on your heat preference.

Enjoy your Korean Style Grilled Cheese (Cheese Tteokbokki)! This fusion dish is perfect for those who love a bit of spice and cheese combined into one delicious meal.

Fried Tofu (Dubujjim)

Ingredients:

- **For the Tofu:**
    - 1 block (14 oz/400g) firm or extra-firm tofu
    - 2-3 tablespoons vegetable oil (for frying)
- **For the Sauce:**
    - 1/4 cup soy sauce
    - 2 tablespoons gochujang (Korean red chili paste)
    - 2 tablespoons sugar or honey
    - 1 tablespoon sesame oil
    - 2 cloves garlic, minced
    - 1 teaspoon minced ginger
    - 1/2 cup water or vegetable broth
    - 1 tablespoon rice vinegar or apple cider vinegar
    - 1 tablespoon corn syrup or honey (optional, for extra sweetness and glossiness)
- **For Garnish:**
    - 1 tablespoon sesame seeds
    - 2-3 green onions, chopped
    - 1/2 teaspoon red pepper flakes (optional, for extra heat)

Instructions:

1. **Prepare the Tofu:**
    - Drain the tofu and press it gently to remove excess moisture. You can use a tofu press or wrap the tofu in a clean kitchen towel and place a heavy object on top to press out the liquid.
    - Cut the tofu into bite-sized cubes.
2. **Fry the Tofu:**
    - Heat the vegetable oil in a non-stick skillet or frying pan over medium-high heat.
    - Add the tofu cubes and fry until they are golden brown and crispy on all sides, about 5-7 minutes. Use a slotted spoon to transfer the fried tofu to a paper towel-lined plate to drain excess oil.
3. **Prepare the Sauce:**
    - In a small bowl, whisk together soy sauce, gochujang, sugar or honey, sesame oil, minced garlic, minced ginger, water or vegetable broth, and vinegar. Add corn syrup or honey if using, and mix until well combined.
4. **Cook the Sauce:**
    - In the same skillet used for frying the tofu, discard any excess oil but keep a small amount in the pan.
    - Pour the prepared sauce into the skillet and bring to a simmer over medium heat.
    - Cook the sauce for about 2-3 minutes until it starts to thicken slightly.
5. **Add the Tofu:**

- Gently add the fried tofu cubes to the skillet with the sauce.
- Stir gently to coat the tofu with the sauce and simmer for an additional 3-5 minutes, allowing the tofu to absorb the flavors.
6. **Garnish and Serve:**
    - Transfer the tofu to a serving dish.
    - Garnish with sesame seeds, chopped green onions, and red pepper flakes (if using).

Tips:

- **Texture:** Firm or extra-firm tofu works best for frying as it holds its shape better.
- **Crispiness:** Ensure the tofu is well-drained and patted dry before frying to achieve a crispy texture.
- **Sauce:** Adjust the sweetness or spiciness of the sauce according to your taste. You can add more gochujang for extra heat or more sugar/honey for added sweetness.

Enjoy your Dubujjim! This Korean fried tofu dish is perfect as a main course or a side dish and is both delicious and nutritious.

Korean Pancake with Seafood (Haemul Jeon)

Ingredients:

- **For the Pancake Batter:**
    - 1 cup all-purpose flour
    - 1/2 cup cornstarch
    - 1 cup cold water
    - 1/2 teaspoon salt
    - 1/2 teaspoon pepper
    - 1 egg (optional, for added richness)
- **For the Filling:**
    - 1/2 cup shrimp, peeled and deveined, chopped
    - 1/2 cup squid, cleaned and chopped
    - 1/2 cup mussels or clams (optional), cleaned and chopped
    - 1/2 cup thinly sliced green onions
    - 1/2 cup thinly sliced carrots
    - 1/2 cup thinly sliced bell peppers (any color)
    - 1/2 cup thinly sliced zucchini
    - 1/2 cup chopped kimchi (optional, for extra flavor)
- **For Cooking:**
    - 2-3 tablespoons vegetable oil
- **For Dipping Sauce (Optional):**
    - 3 tablespoons soy sauce
    - 1 tablespoon rice vinegar or apple cider vinegar
    - 1 teaspoon sesame oil
    - 1 teaspoon sugar
    - 1 teaspoon sesame seeds
    - 1-2 cloves garlic, minced
    - 1 small chili, sliced (optional, for heat)
    - Chopped green onions (optional)

Instructions:

1. **Prepare the Batter:**
    - In a large bowl, whisk together flour, cornstarch, cold water, salt, pepper, and egg (if using) until smooth. The batter should be slightly thick but pourable.
2. **Prepare the Filling:**
    - In another bowl, mix the chopped seafood and vegetables. If using kimchi, add it to the mixture.
3. **Combine Ingredients:**
    - Add the seafood and vegetable mixture to the pancake batter. Stir gently to coat all ingredients evenly.
4. **Cook the Pancake:**

- Heat 1 tablespoon of vegetable oil in a large skillet over medium-high heat.
 - Pour a portion of the batter into the skillet, spreading it out into a round, even layer. The pancake should be about 1/4 to 1/2 inch thick.
 - Cook for about 3-4 minutes on one side, or until the edges are golden brown and crispy. Flip carefully and cook for another 2-3 minutes on the other side.
5. **Serve:**
 - Transfer the cooked pancake to a paper towel-lined plate to drain excess oil.
 - Slice into wedges or bite-sized pieces.
6. **Prepare the Dipping Sauce (Optional):**
 - In a small bowl, mix together soy sauce, rice vinegar, sesame oil, sugar, sesame seeds, minced garlic, and sliced chili. Adjust seasoning to taste.

Tips:

- **Seafood:** Ensure the seafood is well-drained and patted dry before adding it to the batter to avoid excess moisture.
- **Thickness:** Adjust the thickness of the batter by adding more water if needed, but ensure it remains thick enough to hold the seafood and vegetables.
- **Oil:** Add more oil to the skillet as needed to prevent sticking and ensure a crispy texture.

Enjoy your Haemul Jeon! This flavorful Korean seafood pancake is perfect for sharing with family and friends and pairs wonderfully with a side of dipping sauce.

Rice and Kimchi Stir-Fry (Kimchi Bokkeumbap)

Ingredients:

- **For the Stir-Fry:**
    - 2 cups cooked rice (preferably cold or day-old rice)
    - 1 cup kimchi, chopped (with some kimchi juice)
    - 1/2 cup kimchi juice (optional, for extra flavor)
    - 1 tablespoon vegetable oil
    - 1 small onion, diced
    - 2 cloves garlic, minced
    - 1/2 cup diced carrots
    - 1/2 cup diced bell peppers (any color)
    - 1/2 cup chopped green onions (whites and greens separated)
    - 1/2 cup cooked pork, beef, or chicken (optional), diced or shredded
    - 1-2 eggs (optional, for scrambling)
    - 1 tablespoon soy sauce
    - 1 tablespoon gochujang (Korean red chili paste) (optional, for extra spice)
    - 1 teaspoon sesame oil
    - Sesame seeds (for garnish)
    - Additional green onions (for garnish)

Instructions:

1. **Prepare the Ingredients:**
    - Chop the kimchi into bite-sized pieces. If using, chop the cooked meat into small pieces. Dice the vegetables and set aside.
2. **Cook the Vegetables:**
    - Heat vegetable oil in a large skillet or wok over medium-high heat.
    - Add the diced onion and cook until it becomes translucent, about 2-3 minutes.
    - Add the minced garlic and cook for another 30 seconds, or until fragrant.
3. **Add Vegetables and Meat:**
    - Add the diced carrots and bell peppers to the skillet. Cook for about 3-4 minutes until they start to soften.
    - If using cooked meat, add it to the skillet and stir until heated through.
4. **Stir-Fry the Rice:**
    - Add the chopped kimchi and some of the kimchi juice to the skillet. Stir well to combine with the vegetables and meat.
    - Add the cooked rice to the skillet, breaking up any clumps. Stir everything together until the rice is well combined with the kimchi and vegetables.
5. **Season and Finish:**
    - Add soy sauce, gochujang (if using), and sesame oil to the skillet. Stir well to evenly distribute the seasonings.

- **Optional:** Push the rice mixture to one side of the skillet, crack the eggs into the empty space, and scramble them until cooked. Mix the scrambled eggs into the rice.
6. **Garnish and Serve:**
    - Garnish with sesame seeds and additional chopped green onions.
    - Serve hot and enjoy!

Tips:

- **Rice:** Cold or day-old rice works best because it's drier and less likely to become mushy when stir-frying.
- **Kimchi:** The more fermented the kimchi, the more intense the flavor. Adjust the amount based on your taste preference.
- **Spice Level:** Adjust the amount of gochujang and kimchi juice based on how spicy you like your dish.

Enjoy your Kimchi Bokkeumbap! This Korean fried rice is a flavorful and versatile dish that makes a great meal or side.

Korean Breakfast Soup with Noodles (Guksoo)

Ingredients:

- **For the Soup:**
    - 4 cups beef or chicken broth (or water with a beef/chicken bouillon cube)
    - 2 tablespoons soy sauce
    - 1 tablespoon sesame oil
    - 2 cloves garlic, minced
    - 1/2 teaspoon grated ginger (optional)
    - 1/2 lb (225g) beef sirloin or chicken breast, thinly sliced
    - 1 cup mushrooms, sliced (shiitake, oyster, or button mushrooms)
    - 1 small carrot, julienned
    - 1 small zucchini, julienned
    - 1 cup fresh spinach or napa cabbage, chopped
    - 1 package (about 7 oz) Korean noodles (e.g., somyeon or jinjjong-myeon) or any thin noodles
    - 1-2 eggs (optional, for added richness)
    - 1 tablespoon gochujang (Korean red chili paste) or gochugaru (Korean red chili flakes) (optional, for a bit of spice)
- **For Garnish:**
    - 2-3 green onions, chopped
    - 1 tablespoon sesame seeds
    - 1 sheet of nori (seaweed), cut into strips (optional)
    - Pickled radish or kimchi (optional, for serving)

Instructions:

1. **Prepare the Broth:**
    - In a large pot, heat sesame oil over medium heat.
    - Add minced garlic and grated ginger (if using), and sauté for about 30 seconds until fragrant.
    - Add the beef or chicken slices and cook until they start to brown.
2. **Add Broth and Vegetables:**
    - Pour in the beef or chicken broth. If using water, dissolve a bouillon cube in it to make a broth.
    - Bring the mixture to a boil, then reduce the heat to a simmer.
    - Add soy sauce, sliced mushrooms, julienned carrot, and zucchini. Simmer for about 5-7 minutes, or until the vegetables are tender.
3. **Cook the Noodles:**
    - In a separate pot, cook the noodles according to package instructions. Drain and set aside.
4. **Add Spinach and Noodles:**

- Add the chopped spinach or napa cabbage to the simmering broth and cook for another 2 minutes until wilted.
- Gently add the cooked noodles to the pot.
5. **Optional: Add Eggs:**
    - If using eggs, beat them lightly and drizzle them into the soup while stirring gently to create egg ribbons. Cook for another 1-2 minutes until the eggs are cooked through.
6. **Adjust Seasoning:**
    - If desired, add gochujang or gochugaru for a bit of heat. Taste and adjust the seasoning with additional soy sauce or salt if needed.
7. **Serve and Garnish:**
    - Ladle the soup into bowls and garnish with chopped green onions, sesame seeds, and nori strips if using.
    - Serve with pickled radish or kimchi on the side if desired.

Tips:

- **Broth:** For a richer flavor, use homemade beef or chicken broth if you have it. You can also use a combination of water and bouillon cubes as a shortcut.
- **Noodles:** Thin noodles like somyeon or jinjjong-myeon work well for this soup. If you can't find them, any thin pasta or noodle will do.
- **Spice:** Adjust the amount of gochujang or gochugaru according to your spice preference.

Enjoy your Guksoo! This Korean breakfast soup is hearty and nourishing, making it a perfect start to your day or a comforting meal anytime.

Korean Chicken Soup (Samgyetang)

Ingredients:

- **For the Soup:**
    - 1 whole young chicken (about 2-3 lbs), cleaned and trimmed
    - 1/2 cup glutinous rice (sweet rice), rinsed and soaked for 30 minutes
    - 2-3 ginseng roots (dried or fresh, available at Asian markets)
    - 4-5 jujube (Korean dried red dates), pitted
    - 3-4 cloves garlic, peeled
    - 1 small piece of ginger (about 1-inch), peeled and sliced
    - 1 tablespoon Korean ginseng powder (optional, for extra ginseng flavor)
    - 2-3 green onions
    - 1 tablespoon soy sauce (for seasoning the broth)
    - Salt and pepper to taste
    - 8-10 cups water (or enough to cover the chicken)
- **For Garnish (Optional):**
    - Chopped green onions
    - Sesame seeds
    - Sliced garlic

Instructions:

1. **Prepare the Ingredients:**
    - Rinse the glutinous rice under cold water and soak it for about 30 minutes. Drain before use.
    - Clean and trim the chicken, removing any excess fat and patting it dry with paper towels.
2. **Stuff the Chicken:**
    - Stuff the cavity of the chicken with the soaked glutinous rice, ginseng roots, jujube, garlic cloves, and sliced ginger. You can also add a small amount of Korean ginseng powder if desired for extra flavor.
    - Use kitchen twine or toothpicks to secure the cavity if needed.
3. **Prepare the Soup Base:**
    - In a large pot, add enough water to cover the chicken (about 8-10 cups). Bring to a boil over high heat.
    - Once boiling, carefully add the stuffed chicken to the pot. Reduce the heat to medium-low and simmer.
4. **Cook the Soup:**
    - Skim off any foam or impurities that rise to the surface during the first 10-15 minutes of cooking.
    - Add the green onions and continue to simmer for about 1 to 1.5 hours, or until the chicken is tender and fully cooked. The rice inside should be soft and the broth should be rich and flavorful.

5. **Season the Soup:**
    - Once the chicken is cooked, remove it from the pot and let it rest for a few minutes.
    - Season the broth with soy sauce, salt, and pepper to taste. Adjust the seasoning as needed.
6. **Serve:**
    - Place the cooked chicken back into the pot or transfer it to individual serving bowls.
    - Ladle the hot broth over the chicken and garnish with chopped green onions, sesame seeds, and sliced garlic if desired.
    - Serve with steamed rice and kimchi on the side if preferred.

Tips:

- **Rice:** The glutinous rice adds a unique texture to the soup and absorbs the flavors of the broth. Ensure it's well-soaked before stuffing the chicken.
- **Ginseng:** Ginseng adds a distinct flavor and is considered beneficial for health. If you can't find fresh ginseng, dried ginseng or ginseng powder can be used.
- **Cooking Time:** Ensure the chicken is cooked through and the rice is tender. The cooking time may vary based on the size of the chicken.

Enjoy your Samgyetang! This comforting Korean chicken soup is perfect for a nourishing meal and is believed to help boost energy and overall well-being.

Pickled Radish (Kkakdugi)

Ingredients:

- **For the Pickling Brine:**
    - 1 large Korean radish (mu), or 2-3 daikon radishes (about 2 lbs/900g), peeled and cut into small cubes
    - 1/4 cup Korean coarse sea salt (or kosher salt)
    - 1/4 cup sugar
    - 1/4 cup rice vinegar
    - 1 tablespoon soy sauce
    - 1 tablespoon gochugaru (Korean red chili flakes) (adjust to taste)
    - 1 tablespoon minced garlic
    - 1 teaspoon minced ginger
    - 1 tablespoon fish sauce (optional, for added umami)
    - 1-2 green onions, chopped (optional, for garnish)
    - 1 tablespoon sesame seeds (optional, for garnish)

Instructions:

1. **Prepare the Radish:**
    - Peel the radish and cut it into 1/2-inch cubes.
2. **Salt the Radish:**
    - Place the radish cubes in a large bowl and sprinkle with Korean coarse sea salt. Toss to coat the radish evenly with the salt.
    - Let it sit for about 30 minutes. The salt will draw out moisture and help the radish cubes become slightly softened.
3. **Rinse and Drain:**
    - After 30 minutes, rinse the radish cubes under cold water to remove excess salt.
    - Drain well and pat dry with a clean towel or paper towels.
4. **Prepare the Pickling Brine:**
    - In a separate bowl, combine the sugar, rice vinegar, soy sauce, gochugaru, minced garlic, minced ginger, and fish sauce (if using). Stir until the sugar is dissolved and the mixture is well combined.
5. **Combine Radish and Brine:**
    - Add the drained radish cubes to the bowl with the pickling brine. Mix well to ensure all the radish cubes are evenly coated with the brine.
6. **Ferment and Refrigerate:**
    - Transfer the radish mixture to a clean, airtight container or jar. Press the radish down to remove any air bubbles and ensure the liquid covers the radish cubes.
    - Seal the container and refrigerate for at least 24 hours to allow the flavors to develop. The pickled radish can be enjoyed after a day but will improve in flavor as it ferments over time.
7. **Serve:**

- Garnish with chopped green onions and sesame seeds if desired.
- Serve cold as a side dish with Korean meals.

Tips:

- **Radish Type:** Korean radish (mu) has a firmer texture and a slightly different flavor compared to daikon radishes, but daikon can be used as a substitute if necessary.
- **Spice Level:** Adjust the amount of gochugaru based on your heat preference. For a milder flavor, use less gochugaru.
- **Storage:** Kkakdugi can be stored in the refrigerator for up to a month. The flavors will continue to develop and deepen over time.

Enjoy your homemade Kkakdugi! This refreshing and crunchy pickled radish adds a delightful tanginess to your Korean meals and is perfect for balancing richer dishes.

Korean Style Scrambled Eggs (Gyeran Bokkeum)

Ingredients:

- **For the Scrambled Eggs:**
    - 4 large eggs
    - 2 tablespoons milk or water (optional, for fluffier eggs)
    - 1 tablespoon vegetable oil or butter
    - 1 small onion, finely diced
    - 1-2 green onions, chopped
    - 1 small carrot, finely diced (optional, for added texture and color)
    - 1 tablespoon soy sauce
    - 1/2 teaspoon salt (or to taste)
    - 1/4 teaspoon black pepper
    - 1/2 teaspoon sesame oil (optional, for added flavor)
    - Sesame seeds (for garnish, optional)

Instructions:

1. **Prepare the Ingredients:**
    - Crack the eggs into a bowl and whisk them together with the milk or water (if using) until well combined and slightly frothy.
    - Dice the onion and carrot (if using) and chop the green onions.
2. **Cook the Vegetables:**
    - Heat the vegetable oil or butter in a non-stick skillet over medium heat.
    - Add the diced onion and carrot (if using). Sauté until the vegetables are softened and the onion becomes translucent, about 2-3 minutes.
    - Add the chopped green onions and cook for an additional 30 seconds.
3. **Add the Eggs:**
    - Push the vegetables to one side of the skillet. Pour the beaten eggs into the other side of the skillet.
    - Allow the eggs to sit undisturbed for about 30 seconds to start setting.
4. **Scramble the Eggs:**
    - Gently stir the eggs with a spatula, mixing them with the cooked vegetables. Continue to cook and stir until the eggs are cooked through but still soft and fluffy. Be careful not to overcook the eggs; they should be slightly creamy.
5. **Season the Eggs:**
    - Season the scrambled eggs with soy sauce, salt, and black pepper. Stir to combine and adjust seasoning to taste.
    - Drizzle with sesame oil if using, and give it one last gentle stir.
6. **Serve:**
    - Transfer the scrambled eggs to a serving plate.
    - Garnish with sesame seeds if desired.

Tips:

- **Texture:** For fluffier eggs, whisk them well and incorporate air by adding milk or water. This helps create a lighter texture.
- **Heat:** Cook the eggs over medium heat to ensure they cook evenly and avoid burning.
- **Vegetables:** Feel free to add other vegetables like bell peppers or mushrooms based on your preference.

Enjoy your Gyeran Bokkeum! This simple yet tasty Korean-style scrambled eggs dish is perfect for a quick breakfast or as a side dish with your meals.

Spicy Pork Belly (Jeyuk Bokkeum)

Ingredients:

- **For the Pork:**
  - 1 lb (450g) pork belly, thinly sliced
  - 1 tablespoon vegetable oil (for cooking)
- **For the Marinade/Sauce:**
  - 3 tablespoons gochujang (Korean red chili paste)
  - 2 tablespoons gochugaru (Korean red chili flakes) (adjust based on your spice preference)
  - 2 tablespoons soy sauce
  - 1 tablespoon rice wine or mirin
  - 1 tablespoon sugar (or honey)
  - 2 tablespoons sesame oil
  - 4 cloves garlic, minced
  - 1 tablespoon minced ginger
  - 2 tablespoons sesame seeds
  - 1/2 teaspoon black pepper
  - 1 tablespoon ketchup (optional, for a hint of sweetness)
- **For Garnish (Optional):**
  - Chopped green onions
  - Sliced red chili peppers
  - Sesame seeds

Instructions:

1. **Prepare the Pork:**
   - Thinly slice the pork belly into bite-sized pieces. If the pork belly is too fatty, you can trim off some of the excess fat if desired.
2. **Prepare the Marinade/Sauce:**
   - In a bowl, mix together gochujang, gochugaru, soy sauce, rice wine or mirin, sugar or honey, sesame oil, minced garlic, minced ginger, sesame seeds, black pepper, and ketchup (if using). Stir well to combine into a thick sauce.
3. **Marinate the Pork:**
   - Add the sliced pork belly to the bowl with the marinade. Toss to coat the pork evenly with the sauce. Let it marinate for at least 30 minutes to allow the flavors to penetrate the meat. For best results, marinate in the refrigerator for several hours or overnight.
4. **Cook the Pork:**
   - Heat vegetable oil in a large skillet or wok over medium-high heat.
   - Add the marinated pork belly to the skillet in a single layer. Cook, stirring occasionally, until the pork is browned and cooked through, about 7-10 minutes. Ensure the pork is well-coated with the sauce and caramelized.

5. **Garnish and Serve:**
    - Transfer the cooked pork to a serving dish.
    - Garnish with chopped green onions, sliced red chili peppers, and additional sesame seeds if desired.

Tips:

- **Marination:** The longer you marinate the pork, the more flavorful it will be. Try to marinate it for at least 30 minutes, or up to overnight if you have the time.
- **Spice Level:** Adjust the amount of gochujang and gochugaru based on your preference for spiciness.
- **Cooking:** Be careful not to overcrowd the skillet. If necessary, cook the pork in batches to ensure it gets crispy and caramelized.

Enjoy your Jeyuk Bokkeum! This spicy and savory pork belly dish is perfect with steamed rice and can be served as a main course or as part of a Korean-style meal.

Korean Rice Balls (Jumeokbap)

Ingredients:

- **For the Rice Balls:**
    - 2 cups cooked short-grain or medium-grain rice (preferably slightly cold or day-old rice)
    - 1 tablespoon sesame oil
    - 1 tablespoon soy sauce
    - 1 tablespoon sesame seeds
    - 1-2 cloves garlic, minced (optional)
    - 1/4 cup finely chopped kimchi (optional)
    - 1/4 cup chopped spinach or other greens (optional)
    - 1/4 cup finely diced carrots or radish (optional)
    - 1/4 cup cooked and diced meat (beef, chicken, or pork) or tofu (optional)
    - Salt to taste
- **For Garnish (Optional):**
    - Extra sesame seeds
    - Chopped green onions
    - Nori strips (seaweed), cut into thin strips

Instructions:

1. **Prepare the Rice:**
    - Cook the rice according to the package instructions and let it cool slightly. Using slightly cooled or day-old rice helps the rice hold its shape better.
2. **Season the Rice:**
    - In a large bowl, combine the cooked rice with sesame oil, soy sauce, and sesame seeds. Mix well to evenly distribute the seasoning.
    - If using, mix in the minced garlic, chopped kimchi, chopped spinach, diced carrots or radish, and cooked meat or tofu. Adjust the seasoning with salt if needed.
3. **Shape the Rice Balls:**
    - Wet your hands with a little water to prevent the rice from sticking. Take a small portion of the seasoned rice and shape it into a ball or oval shape using your hands. You can also use a small bowl or mold to shape the rice balls if you prefer.
    - If desired, press a small piece of filling, like a piece of kimchi or meat, into the center of the rice before shaping into a ball.
4. **Garnish:**
    - Roll or sprinkle the shaped rice balls with additional sesame seeds, chopped green onions, or nori strips if desired.
5. **Serve:**

- Serve immediately, or store in an airtight container for up to a day at room temperature. For longer storage, keep them in the refrigerator and consume within 2-3 days. Note that rice balls are best enjoyed fresh or at room temperature.

Tips:

- **Rice Texture:** Slightly cooled or day-old rice is easier to work with and helps the rice balls hold their shape better.
- **Customization:** Feel free to customize the rice balls with your favorite fillings or vegetables. Common additions include chopped kimchi, seasoned meat, or vegetables.
- **Shape:** For easier shaping, use a small bowl or rice mold if you have one.

Enjoy your Jumeokbap! These Korean rice balls are versatile and can be made with a variety of ingredients, making them a delicious and handy option for any meal or snack.

Sesame Leaf Pancakes (Kkaennip Jeon)

Ingredients:

- **For the Pancakes:**
    - 15-20 sesame leaves (kkaennip or perilla leaves), washed and dried
    - 1/2 cup all-purpose flour
    - 1/2 cup Korean pancake mix (or use a 1/4 cup flour mixed with a pinch of baking powder and salt)
    - 1/4 cup water (adjust as needed to get the right batter consistency)
    - 1 egg, lightly beaten
    - 1 tablespoon soy sauce
    - 1 tablespoon sesame oil
    - 1 tablespoon vegetable oil (for frying)
- **For the Dipping Sauce (Optional):**
    - 2 tablespoons soy sauce
    - 1 tablespoon rice vinegar
    - 1 teaspoon sesame oil
    - 1 teaspoon sugar or honey
    - 1 clove garlic, minced
    - 1/2 teaspoon gochugaru (Korean red chili flakes) or chopped fresh chili (optional, for heat)
    - 1 tablespoon chopped green onions (optional)

Instructions:

1. **Prepare the Ingredients:**
    - Wash and dry the sesame leaves. If the leaves are large, you can cut them in half or trim them to fit your frying pan.
    - In a bowl, mix the flour, Korean pancake mix (or flour + baking powder), and a pinch of salt.
2. **Prepare the Batter:**
    - Add water to the dry ingredients gradually, mixing until you get a smooth batter. The batter should be slightly thick but not too heavy. Adjust the water amount as needed.
    - Stir in the beaten egg, soy sauce, and sesame oil until well combined.
3. **Coat the Leaves:**
    - Heat vegetable oil in a large skillet over medium heat.
    - Dip each sesame leaf into the batter, ensuring both sides are coated.
4. **Fry the Pancakes:**
    - Place the coated sesame leaves in the hot skillet. Fry until golden brown and crispy on both sides, about 2-3 minutes per side. You can cook multiple leaves at once, but avoid overcrowding the pan.
5. **Drain and Serve:**

- Transfer the cooked pancakes to a plate lined with paper towels to drain excess oil.
- Serve warm with dipping sauce if desired.

Dipping Sauce:

1. **Mix the Sauce:**
    - In a small bowl, combine soy sauce, rice vinegar, sesame oil, sugar or honey, minced garlic, gochugaru (if using), and chopped green onions.
    - Stir until the sugar or honey is dissolved and all ingredients are well combined.
2. **Serve:**
    - Serve the dipping sauce alongside the sesame leaf pancakes for dipping.

Tips:

- **Consistency:** The batter should be thick enough to coat the leaves without dripping off too much. Adjust the water or flour to achieve the right consistency.
- **Oil:** Use enough oil to cover the bottom of the skillet, ensuring even frying and crispiness.
- **Dipping Sauce:** Adjust the ingredients in the dipping sauce to suit your taste, adding more or less garlic, sugar, or chili flakes as desired.

Enjoy your Kkaennip Jeon! These sesame leaf pancakes are a fragrant and savory treat that pairs well with a variety of Korean dishes or can be enjoyed on their own.

Korean BBQ Breakfast Bowl

Ingredients:

- **For the Korean BBQ Meat:**
    - 1 lb (450g) beef sirloin or pork belly, thinly sliced
    - 2 tablespoons soy sauce
    - 2 tablespoons brown sugar or honey
    - 1 tablespoon sesame oil
    - 2 cloves garlic, minced
    - 1 teaspoon grated ginger
    - 1 tablespoon gochujang (Korean red chili paste) (optional, for a touch of heat)
    - 1 tablespoon rice wine or mirin (optional)
- **For the Breakfast Bowl:**
    - 2 cups cooked white or brown rice (preferably slightly warm or at room temperature)
    - 1 cup spinach or mixed greens
    - 1 cup thinly sliced vegetables (such as carrots, bell peppers, or cucumbers)
    - 4 eggs
    - 2 tablespoons vegetable oil or butter (for frying eggs)
    - Sesame seeds (for garnish)
    - Sliced green onions (for garnish)
    - Kimchi (for serving, optional)

Instructions:

1. **Marinate the Meat:**
    - In a bowl, combine soy sauce, brown sugar or honey, sesame oil, minced garlic, grated ginger, gochujang (if using), and rice wine or mirin (if using). Mix well.
    - Add the thinly sliced beef or pork to the marinade and toss to coat evenly. Marinate for at least 30 minutes, or up to overnight in the refrigerator for more flavor.
2. **Cook the Meat:**
    - Heat a large skillet or grill pan over medium-high heat.
    - Add the marinated meat to the skillet in a single layer. Cook for about 3-4 minutes per side, or until fully cooked and slightly caramelized. Remove from heat and set aside.
3. **Prepare the Vegetables:**
    - If using raw vegetables like carrots or bell peppers, you can sauté them lightly in the same skillet used for the meat, or leave them raw for a crunchy texture.
    - Blanch the spinach or greens in boiling water for a minute, then drain and set aside.
4. **Fry the Eggs:**
    - Heat vegetable oil or butter in a non-stick skillet over medium heat.

- Crack the eggs into the skillet and cook until the whites are set but the yolks are still runny, about 2-3 minutes. You can cook the eggs sunny-side up or over-easy, depending on your preference.
5. **Assemble the Breakfast Bowl:**
   - Divide the cooked rice between bowls.
   - Arrange the cooked Korean BBQ meat, blanched spinach or greens, and sliced vegetables on top of the rice.
   - Place a fried egg on top of each bowl.
   - Garnish with sesame seeds and sliced green onions.
6. **Serve:**
   - Serve the Korean BBQ Breakfast Bowl warm. You can also add a side of kimchi for extra flavor and texture.

Tips:

- **Marination:** Marinating the meat for several hours or overnight enhances the flavor, so plan ahead if possible.
- **Rice:** Use freshly cooked rice for the best texture, or reheat leftover rice if needed.
- **Vegetables:** Customize the vegetables based on your preference and what you have on hand. Roasted vegetables can also be a great addition.
- **Eggs:** Adjust the doneness of the eggs based on your preference. For a more runny yolk, cook the eggs sunny-side up.

Enjoy your Korean BBQ Breakfast Bowl! This dish brings together the savory flavors of Korean BBQ with the comforting elements of a breakfast bowl, making it a delicious and satisfying meal for any time of day.

Sweet and Savory Soybean Soup (Doenjang Guk)

Ingredients:

- **For the Soup:**
    - 1/4 cup doenjang (Korean soybean paste)
    - 4 cups water or beef/chicken stock
    - 1 small onion, sliced
    - 1-2 cloves garlic, minced
    - 1 small zucchini, sliced
    - 1 cup mushrooms (shiitake, oyster, or button), sliced
    - 1 medium potato, peeled and cubed
    - 1/2 cup tofu, cubed
    - 1 tablespoon soy sauce (optional, for extra seasoning)
    - 1 tablespoon sesame oil
    - Salt and pepper to taste
    - 1-2 green onions, chopped (for garnish)
    - 1-2 tablespoons sesame seeds (for garnish)

Instructions:

1. **Prepare the Soup Base:**
    - In a large pot, heat sesame oil over medium heat.
    - Add the sliced onion and minced garlic. Sauté until the onion becomes translucent and fragrant, about 2-3 minutes.
2. **Add Water or Stock:**
    - Pour in the water or beef/chicken stock. Bring to a boil, then reduce heat and let it simmer.
3. **Incorporate Doenjang:**
    - Scoop out the doenjang paste and dissolve it in a small amount of hot soup broth, stirring until smooth. Add the dissolved doenjang to the pot.
    - Stir well to incorporate the doenjang into the broth.
4. **Add Vegetables and Tofu:**
    - Add the cubed potatoes, sliced zucchini, and mushrooms to the pot.
    - Simmer the soup for about 10-15 minutes, or until the vegetables are tender.
5. **Add Tofu:**
    - Gently add the cubed tofu to the pot and simmer for an additional 5 minutes to heat through and allow the tofu to absorb the flavors.
6. **Season the Soup:**
    - Taste the soup and adjust the seasoning with soy sauce, salt, and pepper as needed.
7. **Garnish and Serve:**
    - Ladle the soup into bowls.
    - Garnish with chopped green onions and sesame seeds.

- Serve hot with steamed rice and kimchi on the side if desired.

Tips:

- **Doenjang:** Use high-quality doenjang for the best flavor. It can be found in Korean or Asian grocery stores.
- **Vegetables:** Customize the vegetables based on what you have on hand. Common additions include Korean radish or carrots.
- **Tofu:** For a firmer texture, use extra-firm tofu and press it to remove excess moisture before cubing.

Enjoy your Doenjang Guk! This hearty and flavorful Korean soybean soup is perfect for a comforting meal and pairs wonderfully with rice and other Korean side dishes.

Braised Chicken (Dakjjim)

Ingredients:

- **For the Braised Chicken:**
    - 2 lbs (900g) chicken (legs, thighs, or a mix), cut into pieces
    - 1 tablespoon vegetable oil
    - 1 onion, sliced
    - 2-3 cloves garlic, minced
    - 1 small piece of ginger (about 1 inch), minced
    - 2 carrots, cut into chunks
    - 1 medium potato, peeled and cut into chunks
    - 1 cup shiitake mushrooms or other mushrooms, sliced (optional)
    - 1/4 cup soy sauce
    - 1/4 cup rice wine or mirin
    - 1/4 cup brown sugar or honey
    - 1 tablespoon gochujang (Korean red chili paste) (optional, for a touch of heat)
    - 1 tablespoon sesame oil
    - 1 cup water or chicken stock
    - 1-2 green onions, chopped (for garnish)
    - Sesame seeds (for garnish)

Instructions:

1. **Prepare the Chicken:**
    - If you're using bone-in chicken, you may want to blanch it first to remove excess impurities. To do this, bring a pot of water to a boil, add the chicken pieces, and cook for 5 minutes. Drain and rinse the chicken under cold water.
2. **Sauté Aromatics:**
    - Heat vegetable oil in a large pot or Dutch oven over medium heat.
    - Add the sliced onion, minced garlic, and minced ginger. Sauté until the onion becomes translucent and fragrant, about 3-4 minutes.
3. **Brown the Chicken:**
    - Add the chicken pieces to the pot and cook until they are lightly browned on all sides, about 5-7 minutes.
4. **Add Vegetables:**
    - Add the carrots, potatoes, and mushrooms (if using) to the pot. Stir to combine.
5. **Prepare the Sauce:**
    - In a bowl, mix together soy sauce, rice wine or mirin, brown sugar or honey, and gochujang (if using). Stir until the sugar is dissolved.
6. **Add Sauce and Simmer:**
    - Pour the sauce mixture over the chicken and vegetables. Add sesame oil and water or chicken stock.

- Bring the mixture to a boil, then reduce the heat to low. Cover and simmer for about 30-40 minutes, or until the chicken is cooked through and the vegetables are tender. Stir occasionally and check the sauce level, adding more water or stock if necessary.
7. **Adjust Seasoning:**
    - Taste the sauce and adjust the seasoning if needed. You can add a bit more soy sauce for saltiness or sugar for sweetness.
8. **Garnish and Serve:**
    - Transfer the braised chicken and vegetables to a serving dish.
    - Garnish with chopped green onions and sesame seeds.
    - Serve hot with steamed rice.

Tips:

- **Chicken:** Bone-in chicken pieces give more flavor, but boneless chicken can be used if preferred.
- **Vegetables:** Feel free to add other vegetables like bell peppers, Korean radish, or onions based on your preference.
- **Sauce:** Adjust the level of sweetness and spiciness to suit your taste. The gochujang can be omitted for a milder flavor.

Enjoy your Dakjjim! This savory and comforting Korean braised chicken dish is perfect for a cozy family meal and pairs wonderfully with steamed rice and kimchi.

Korean Kimchi Omelette

Ingredients:

- **For the Kimchi Omelette:**
    - 3 large eggs
    - 1/2 cup kimchi, chopped (with some of the juice if desired)
    - 1 small onion, finely chopped
    - 1 small green bell pepper, finely chopped (optional)
    - 1-2 cloves garlic, minced
    - 1 tablespoon vegetable oil or butter (for cooking)
    - 1 tablespoon soy sauce (optional, for additional seasoning)
    - 1/4 teaspoon black pepper
    - 1/4 cup shredded cheese (cheddar, mozzarella, or your choice, optional)
    - Chopped green onions (for garnish)
    - Sesame seeds (for garnish)

Instructions:

1. **Prepare the Ingredients:**
    - Chop the kimchi into small pieces. If it's very juicy, you might want to drain some of the liquid to prevent the omelette from becoming too watery.
    - Finely chop the onion and green bell pepper (if using). Mince the garlic.
2. **Sauté Vegetables:**
    - Heat vegetable oil or butter in a non-stick skillet over medium heat.
    - Add the chopped onion, green bell pepper (if using), and minced garlic. Sauté until the vegetables are softened and the onion is translucent, about 3-4 minutes.
3. **Add Kimchi:**
    - Add the chopped kimchi to the skillet and cook for another 2-3 minutes, allowing it to heat through and combine with the vegetables.
4. **Prepare the Egg Mixture:**
    - In a bowl, beat the eggs and season with black pepper and soy sauce (if using). You can also add a pinch of salt if desired, but be cautious as kimchi is already salty.
5. **Cook the Omelette:**
    - Pour the beaten eggs over the kimchi and vegetable mixture in the skillet. Let it cook undisturbed for about 1-2 minutes until the edges start to set.
    - Gently lift the edges of the omelette with a spatula and tilt the skillet to allow any uncooked egg to flow to the edges.
6. **Add Cheese (Optional):**
    - If using cheese, sprinkle it over one half of the omelette when the eggs are almost fully set.
7. **Fold and Serve:**

- Once the eggs are mostly set and the cheese is melted (if using), fold the omelette in half over the filling.
- Cook for another 1-2 minutes, or until the omelette is cooked through and slightly golden brown.

8. **Garnish:**
    - Transfer the omelette to a plate.
    - Garnish with chopped green onions and sesame seeds.

Tips:

- **Kimchi:** Use well-fermented kimchi for the best flavor. If the kimchi is very spicy, adjust the amount according to your taste.
- **Cheese:** Cheese is optional but adds a creamy texture and extra flavor. Use your favorite type or omit it for a lighter version.
- **Serving:** This omelette is delicious on its own or served with a side of steamed rice or fresh salad.

Enjoy your Korean Kimchi Omelette! This dish combines the bold flavors of kimchi with the comfort of a classic omelette, making it a tasty and unique addition to your breakfast or brunch menu.

Red Bean Soup (Pat Juk)

Ingredients:

- **For the Red Bean Soup:**
    - 1 cup adzuki beans (red beans)
    - 4 cups water
    - 1/2 cup sugar (adjust to taste, you can use brown sugar or honey instead)
    - 1/4 teaspoon salt
    - 1 tablespoon sesame oil (optional, for flavor)
- **For Garnish (Optional):**
    - Chopped pine nuts
    - Sliced jujube (dried red dates)
    - Sesame seeds

Instructions:

1. **Prepare the Beans:**
    - Rinse the adzuki beans under cold water to remove any dirt or debris.
    - Soak the beans in water for 4-6 hours or overnight. This helps to soften the beans and reduce cooking time.
2. **Cook the Beans:**
    - Drain the soaked beans and place them in a large pot.
    - Add 4 cups of water and bring to a boil over high heat.
    - Reduce the heat to low, cover, and simmer for 40-50 minutes, or until the beans are tender. Stir occasionally and add more water if necessary to keep the beans covered.
3. **Make the Bean Paste:**
    - Once the beans are cooked and tender, you can either mash them slightly with a spoon or use an immersion blender to partially puree the beans. If you prefer a smoother texture, blend until you reach your desired consistency.
    - If you prefer a smoother soup, you can also strain the bean mixture through a fine-mesh sieve to remove the skins.
4. **Sweeten and Season:**
    - Stir in the sugar and salt. Adjust the sweetness to your liking. If you're using honey, add it after removing the pot from heat to preserve its flavor.
    - Stir in sesame oil if using for added flavor.
5. **Serve:**
    - Ladle the red bean soup into bowls.
    - Garnish with chopped pine nuts, sliced jujube, and sesame seeds if desired.

Tips:

- **Beans:** Using adzuki beans is traditional, but other types of red beans can also be used.

- **Texture:** Adjust the texture of the soup to your preference by blending more or less of the beans.
- **Sweetener:** You can use different types of sweeteners such as brown sugar, honey, or even maple syrup.

Enjoy your Pat Juk! This sweet and hearty red bean soup is a traditional Korean comfort food that's both nutritious and satisfying.

Stir-Fried Cabbage (Baechu Bokkeum)

Ingredients:

- **For the Stir-Fried Cabbage:**
    - 1 medium cabbage, sliced into thin strips
    - 2 tablespoons vegetable oil or sesame oil
    - 3 cloves garlic, minced
    - 1 small onion, sliced
    - 1 small carrot, julienned (optional)
    - 2-3 tablespoons soy sauce
    - 1 tablespoon gochujang (Korean red chili paste) (optional, for heat)
    - 1 tablespoon sugar or honey
    - 1 tablespoon sesame seeds
    - 2-3 green onions, chopped (for garnish)
    - Salt and pepper to taste

Instructions:

1. **Prepare the Cabbage:**
    - Slice the cabbage into thin strips. If the cabbage is large, you might want to cut it into halves or quarters before slicing.
2. **Heat the Oil:**
    - Heat the vegetable oil or sesame oil in a large skillet or wok over medium-high heat.
3. **Sauté Aromatics:**
    - Add the minced garlic and sliced onion to the skillet. Sauté until the onion becomes translucent and the garlic is fragrant, about 2-3 minutes.
4. **Add Vegetables:**
    - Add the sliced cabbage and julienned carrot (if using) to the skillet. Stir-fry for about 5-7 minutes, or until the cabbage is tender but still crisp.
5. **Add Seasonings:**
    - Stir in the soy sauce, gochujang (if using), and sugar or honey. Continue to stir-fry for another 2-3 minutes, allowing the flavors to meld and the cabbage to absorb the seasonings.
6. **Adjust Flavor:**
    - Taste and adjust the seasoning with salt and pepper as needed.
7. **Garnish and Serve:**
    - Sprinkle the stir-fried cabbage with sesame seeds and chopped green onions.
    - Serve warm as a side dish with rice or as part of a Korean meal.

Tips:

- **Cabbage:** You can use Napa cabbage for a more traditional texture, but regular green cabbage works well too.
- **Spiciness:** Adjust the amount of gochujang based on your spice preference. You can omit it for a milder version.
- **Texture:** For extra crunch, consider adding some chopped bell peppers or other vegetables.

Enjoy your Baechu Bokkeum! This simple and flavorful stir-fried cabbage is a great addition to any meal, bringing a touch of Korean flavor to your table.

Korean Hotteok (Sweet Pancakes)

Ingredients:

- **For the Dough:**
    - 2 1/4 teaspoons active dry yeast (1 packet)
    - 1/2 cup warm water (110°F or 45°C)
    - 1 tablespoon sugar
    - 2 cups all-purpose flour
    - 1/4 teaspoon salt
    - 1 tablespoon vegetable oil
    - 1/4 cup milk (room temperature)
- **For the Filling:**
    - 1/2 cup brown sugar
    - 1 teaspoon ground cinnamon
    - 1/4 cup chopped nuts (such as walnuts, peanuts, or almonds)
    - 1 tablespoon sesame seeds (optional)
- **For Cooking:**
    - Vegetable oil or butter for frying

Instructions:

1. **Prepare the Dough:**
    - In a small bowl, dissolve the yeast and sugar in warm water. Let it sit for about 5-10 minutes, or until it becomes frothy.
    - In a large bowl, combine the flour and salt. Make a well in the center and pour in the yeast mixture, milk, and vegetable oil.
    - Mix until a dough forms. Knead the dough on a lightly floured surface for about 5-7 minutes, or until it becomes smooth and elastic.
    - Place the dough in a lightly oiled bowl, cover it with a damp cloth or plastic wrap, and let it rise in a warm place for about 1 hour, or until it has doubled in size.
2. **Prepare the Filling:**
    - In a small bowl, mix together the brown sugar, ground cinnamon, chopped nuts, and sesame seeds (if using). Set aside.
3. **Shape the Pancakes:**
    - Punch down the risen dough and divide it into 8-10 equal pieces.
    - Flatten each piece of dough into a small disc using your hands or a rolling pin.
    - Place a spoonful of the filling in the center of each disc.
    - Carefully fold the edges of the dough over the filling and pinch to seal, forming a ball. Flatten the filled dough slightly to form a pancake shape.
4. **Cook the Hotteok:**
    - Heat a non-stick skillet or griddle over medium heat and lightly grease it with vegetable oil or butter.

- Place the pancakes in the skillet and cook for about 2-3 minutes on each side, or until golden brown and crispy. Press down gently with a spatula to ensure even cooking and to help the filling melt inside.
- You may need to adjust the heat to ensure that the pancakes cook evenly without burning.

5. **Serve:**
   - Transfer the cooked hotteok to a plate and let them cool slightly. They are best enjoyed warm when the filling is still gooey.

Tips:

- **Dough Consistency:** The dough should be slightly sticky but manageable. If it's too sticky, add a little more flour; if it's too dry, add a bit more milk.
- **Filling Variations:** Feel free to customize the filling with ingredients like chocolate chips or dried fruit if you like.
- **Cooking:** Ensure the heat isn't too high to avoid burning the outside while leaving the inside uncooked.

Enjoy your Hotteok! These sweet and warm Korean pancakes are a delightful treat, perfect for a cozy snack or dessert.

Pork and Vegetable Soup (Dwaeji Guk)

Ingredients:

- **For the Soup:**
    - 1 lb (450g) pork belly or pork shoulder, cut into bite-sized pieces
    - 1 tablespoon vegetable oil
    - 1 small onion, chopped
    - 2-3 cloves garlic, minced
    - 1 small piece of ginger (about 1 inch), minced
    - 1 medium carrot, sliced
    - 1 cup mushrooms (shiitake, oyster, or button), sliced
    - 1 small potato, peeled and diced
    - 2 tablespoons soy sauce
    - 1 tablespoon gochujang (Korean red chili paste) (optional, for heat)
    - 1 tablespoon sesame oil
    - 4 cups water or chicken stock
    - 1 tablespoon Korean chili flakes (gochugaru) (optional, for extra spice)
    - Salt and pepper to taste
    - Chopped green onions (for garnish)
    - Sesame seeds (for garnish)

Instructions:

1. **Prepare the Pork:**
    - Heat the vegetable oil in a large pot or Dutch oven over medium-high heat.
    - Add the pork pieces and cook until they are browned on all sides, about 5-7 minutes.
2. **Sauté Aromatics:**
    - Add the chopped onion, minced garlic, and minced ginger to the pot. Sauté until the onion becomes translucent and fragrant, about 3 minutes.
3. **Add Vegetables:**
    - Add the sliced carrot, mushrooms, and diced potato to the pot. Stir to combine with the pork and aromatics.
4. **Season and Simmer:**
    - Stir in the soy sauce, gochujang (if using), sesame oil, and Korean chili flakes (if using). Mix well to coat the ingredients with the seasonings.
    - Pour in the water or chicken stock. Bring to a boil, then reduce the heat to low and simmer for about 30-40 minutes, or until the pork and vegetables are tender.
5. **Adjust Seasoning:**
    - Taste the soup and adjust the seasoning with salt and pepper as needed.
6. **Garnish and Serve:**
    - Ladle the soup into bowls.
    - Garnish with chopped green onions and sesame seeds.

Tips:

- **Pork:** Pork belly is commonly used for its rich flavor, but pork shoulder or any cut of pork that you prefer can also be used.
- **Vegetables:** Feel free to customize the vegetables based on what you have on hand or your personal preference. Other vegetables like Korean radish or bell peppers can be added.
- **Spice Level:** Adjust the amount of gochujang and Korean chili flakes according to your spice preference. You can omit them for a milder version.

Enjoy your Dwaeji Guk! This hearty Korean pork and vegetable soup is perfect for a cozy meal and pairs well with steamed rice or kimchi.

Spicy Rice Cake (Tteokbokki)

Ingredients:

- **For the Tteokbokki:**
    - 1 lb (450g) Korean rice cakes (tteokbokki tteok) or oval-shaped rice cakes
    - 2 cups water or chicken stock
    - 1/4 cup gochujang (Korean red chili paste)
    - 2 tablespoons gochugaru (Korean red chili flakes) (adjust to taste)
    - 2 tablespoons soy sauce
    - 1 tablespoon sugar or honey
    - 1 tablespoon sesame oil
    - 2 cloves garlic, minced
    - 1 small onion, thinly sliced
    - 1 small carrot, julienned (optional)
    - 1 cup cabbage, chopped (optional)
    - 1-2 green onions, chopped (for garnish)
    - Sesame seeds (for garnish)
    - Fish cakes (eomuk) or sliced hot dogs (optional, for added protein)

Instructions:

1. **Prepare the Rice Cakes:**
    - If using frozen rice cakes, soak them in warm water for about 30 minutes to thaw and soften. Drain before cooking.
    - Fresh rice cakes can be used directly without soaking.
2. **Make the Sauce:**
    - In a bowl, mix together gochujang, gochugaru, soy sauce, and sugar or honey. Stir until well combined and set aside.
3. **Cook the Aromatics:**
    - Heat sesame oil in a large pan or skillet over medium heat.
    - Add the minced garlic and sliced onion. Sauté until the onion becomes translucent and fragrant, about 2-3 minutes.
4. **Add the Sauce:**
    - Stir in the sauce mixture and cook for another 1-2 minutes to let the flavors meld.
5. **Add Water or Stock:**
    - Pour in the water or chicken stock. Bring to a simmer.
6. **Add Rice Cakes and Vegetables:**
    - Add the soaked rice cakes to the pan. If using fish cakes or hot dogs, add them now.
    - Add the julienned carrots and chopped cabbage (if using).
7. **Simmer:**

- Cook, stirring occasionally, for about 10-15 minutes, or until the rice cakes are heated through and the sauce has thickened to a glossy consistency. The rice cakes should become tender and absorb the sauce.
8. **Garnish and Serve:**
    - Transfer the Tteokbokki to a serving dish.
    - Garnish with chopped green onions and sesame seeds.
    - Serve hot, ideally with a side of kimchi or pickled radish.

Tips:

- **Spice Level:** Adjust the amount of gochujang and gochugaru based on your preference for spiciness. You can also use less gochugaru if you prefer a milder dish.
- **Texture:** If the sauce gets too thick, you can add a bit more water or stock to reach your desired consistency.
- **Protein Additions:** Fish cakes (eomuk) are a common addition and add a savory depth to the dish. Hot dogs can also be used for a different twist.

Enjoy your Tteokbokki! This spicy and chewy Korean rice cake dish is a deliciously addictive treat that's perfect for snacking or as a hearty meal.

Korean Egg Drop Soup (Gyeran Guk)

Ingredients:

- **For the Soup:**
    - 4 cups chicken broth or water
    - 2 large eggs
    - 1 tablespoon soy sauce
    - 1 teaspoon sesame oil
    - 1/2 teaspoon salt (adjust to taste)
    - 1/4 teaspoon black pepper
    - 1 small onion, thinly sliced
    - 1 small zucchini, thinly sliced or julienned (optional)
    - 1/2 cup mushrooms, sliced (shiitake or button mushrooms, optional)
    - 1-2 green onions, chopped (for garnish)
    - Sesame seeds (for garnish)

Instructions:

1. **Prepare the Broth:**
    - In a medium pot, bring the chicken broth or water to a boil over medium-high heat.
2. **Cook the Vegetables:**
    - Add the sliced onion, zucchini (if using), and mushrooms (if using) to the pot. Cook for about 5 minutes, or until the vegetables are tender.
3. **Season the Soup:**
    - Stir in the soy sauce, sesame oil, salt, and black pepper. Adjust seasoning to taste.
4. **Prepare the Eggs:**
    - In a small bowl, beat the eggs until well combined.
5. **Add the Eggs:**
    - Reduce the heat to low and slowly pour the beaten eggs into the pot while stirring gently. This will create egg ribbons or strands in the soup.
6. **Simmer:**
    - Let the soup simmer for another 1-2 minutes, allowing the eggs to fully cook and form soft strands.
7. **Garnish and Serve:**
    - Ladle the soup into bowls.
    - Garnish with chopped green onions and sesame seeds.

Tips:

- **Broth:** You can use chicken broth for more flavor or water for a lighter version. Homemade broth adds the best flavor, but store-bought works well too.

- **Vegetables:** Customize the vegetables according to your preference. Korean radish, bell peppers, or spinach can be used as alternatives.
- **Eggs:** Pour the beaten eggs slowly and stir gently to create delicate egg ribbons.

Enjoy your Gyeran Guk! This Korean Egg Drop Soup is a warm and comforting option that's perfect for a light meal or as part of a larger Korean spread.

Mung Bean Pancakes (Bindaetteok)

Ingredients:

- **For the Pancake Batter:**
    - 1 cup dried mung beans
    - 2-3 cups water (for soaking and blending)
    - 1/2 cup kimchi, chopped (optional, for extra flavor)
    - 1/2 cup cooked pork (optional, finely chopped; can also use beef or omit)
    - 1 small onion, finely chopped
    - 1 small carrot, finely chopped
    - 2-3 cloves garlic, minced
    - 2-3 green onions, chopped
    - 1 tablespoon soy sauce
    - 1 teaspoon salt (adjust to taste)
    - 1/2 teaspoon black pepper
    - 1/4 teaspoon gochugaru (Korean red chili flakes) (optional, for heat)
    - 1 egg (optional, for binding)
- **For Cooking:**
    - Vegetable oil or sesame oil (for frying)
- **For Dipping Sauce:**
    - 2 tablespoons soy sauce
    - 1 tablespoon vinegar
    - 1 teaspoon sugar
    - 1 clove garlic, minced
    - 1/2 teaspoon sesame seeds
    - 1 green onion, finely chopped

Instructions:

1. **Prepare the Mung Beans:**
    - Rinse the mung beans under cold water. Soak them in a bowl of water for at least 4 hours or overnight.
2. **Make the Batter:**
    - Drain the soaked mung beans and place them in a blender or food processor.
    - Add 2 cups of water and blend until the beans are finely ground and the mixture is smooth. If necessary, add a little more water to achieve a pancake batter consistency.
3. **Mix in Vegetables and Meat:**
    - Transfer the mung bean batter to a large bowl.
    - Stir in the chopped kimchi (if using), cooked pork (or other meat), onion, carrot, garlic, green onions, soy sauce, salt, black pepper, and gochugaru (if using).
    - If the batter seems too thin, you can add a bit of flour to thicken it. You can also mix in an egg for better binding, but this is optional.

4. **Cook the Pancakes:**
    - Heat a large skillet or griddle over medium-high heat and add a generous amount of vegetable oil or sesame oil.
    - Spoon a portion of the batter into the skillet, spreading it out into a thin, even pancake. You can make them small or large depending on your preference.
    - Cook for about 3-4 minutes on each side, or until the pancakes are golden brown and crispy. Flip carefully to avoid breaking.
5. **Prepare the Dipping Sauce:**
    - In a small bowl, mix together soy sauce, vinegar, sugar, minced garlic, sesame seeds, and chopped green onion.
6. **Serve:**
    - Transfer the cooked pancakes to a plate lined with paper towels to drain excess oil.
    - Serve hot with the dipping sauce on the side.

Tips:

- **Consistency:** The batter should be thick enough to hold together but not too dry. Adjust with water or flour as needed.
- **Frying:** Make sure the oil is hot enough before adding the batter to get crispy pancakes. Too little oil can make them stick to the pan.
- **Vegetables and Meat:** Customize the ingredients according to your preference. You can use different vegetables or add other proteins.

Enjoy your Bindaetteok! These mung bean pancakes are crispy, savory, and packed with flavor, making them a perfect snack or appetizer for any occasion.

Noodle Soup (Jajangmyeon)

Ingredients:

- **For the Sauce:**
    - 1/2 cup jajangmyeon sauce (black bean paste, or **chunjang**)
    - 1 tablespoon vegetable oil
    - 1/2 lb (225g) pork belly or pork shoulder, diced
    - 1 small onion, diced
    - 1 small zucchini, diced
    - 1 small carrot, diced
    - 1 cup cabbage, shredded
    - 2 cloves garlic, minced
    - 1 tablespoon soy sauce
    - 1 tablespoon sugar
    - 1 cup water or chicken broth
    - 1 tablespoon cornstarch mixed with 2 tablespoons water (for thickening)
- **For the Noodles:**
    - 8 oz (225g) fresh or dried jajangmyeon noodles (or substitute with Chinese egg noodles or other preferred noodles)
- **For Garnish:**
    - 1 cucumber, julienned
    - Chopped green onions

Instructions:

1. **Prepare the Noodles:**
    - Cook the noodles according to the package instructions. Drain and set aside.
2. **Make the Sauce:**
    - Heat vegetable oil in a large pan or wok over medium-high heat.
    - Add the diced pork and cook until it starts to brown, about 5 minutes.
    - Add the diced onion, zucchini, carrot, and cabbage. Stir-fry for 3-4 minutes, or until the vegetables start to soften.
    - Stir in the minced garlic and cook for another minute.
3. **Add the Bean Paste:**
    - Push the pork and vegetables to one side of the pan and add the black bean paste (chunjang) to the empty side. Stir-fry the paste for 1-2 minutes to enhance its flavor.
4. **Combine Ingredients:**
    - Mix the bean paste with the pork and vegetables. Stir in the soy sauce, sugar, and water or chicken broth.
    - Bring to a boil, then reduce the heat and let it simmer for about 5 minutes.
5. **Thicken the Sauce:**

- Stir in the cornstarch mixture. Continue to cook for another 2-3 minutes, or until the sauce thickens.
6. **Combine with Noodles:**
    - Add the cooked noodles to the sauce and stir to coat the noodles evenly with the sauce.
7. **Serve:**
    - Divide the noodles and sauce among serving bowls.
    - Garnish with julienned cucumber and chopped green onions.

Tips:

- **Bean Paste:** Jajangmyeon sauce (chunjang) can be found in Korean or Asian grocery stores. It's a key ingredient for the authentic flavor.
- **Vegetables:** Feel free to adjust the vegetables according to your taste or what you have on hand.
- **Thickness:** Adjust the thickness of the sauce by adding more or less cornstarch mixture as needed.

Enjoy your Jajangmyeon! This classic Korean noodle dish is a hearty and flavorful option that's perfect for a satisfying meal.

Grilled Vegetables (Yachae Gui)

Ingredients:

- **For the Vegetables:**
    - 1 medium zucchini, sliced into thick rounds or half-moons
    - 1 red bell pepper, cut into chunks
    - 1 yellow bell pepper, cut into chunks
    - 1 cup mushrooms (shiitake, cremini, or button), cleaned and stems trimmed
    - 1 small red onion, cut into wedges
    - 1 medium carrot, peeled and cut into thin strips or rounds
    - 1 tablespoon vegetable oil or sesame oil
    - Salt and pepper to taste
- **For the Marinade (optional):**
    - 2 tablespoons soy sauce
    - 1 tablespoon sesame oil
    - 1 tablespoon honey or sugar
    - 1-2 cloves garlic, minced
    - 1 teaspoon ginger, minced
    - 1 tablespoon rice vinegar or apple cider vinegar
    - 1 teaspoon sesame seeds (optional)
    - 1-2 green onions, chopped (for garnish)
- **For the Dipping Sauce (optional):**
    - 2 tablespoons soy sauce
    - 1 tablespoon rice vinegar
    - 1 teaspoon sugar
    - 1 clove garlic, minced
    - 1 teaspoon sesame seeds
    - 1 green onion, finely chopped
    - 1/2 teaspoon gochugaru (Korean red chili flakes) (optional, for heat)

Instructions:

1. **Prepare the Vegetables:**
    - Wash and cut the vegetables into even-sized pieces to ensure uniform grilling.
2. **Marinate (Optional):**
    - If marinating, mix the soy sauce, sesame oil, honey or sugar, minced garlic, minced ginger, rice vinegar, and sesame seeds in a bowl.
    - Toss the vegetables in the marinade and let them sit for at least 15 minutes, or up to 1 hour for more flavor.
3. **Preheat the Grill:**
    - Preheat your grill to medium-high heat. If using a grill pan, preheat it over medium heat on the stovetop.
4. **Grill the Vegetables:**

- Brush the vegetables with vegetable oil or sesame oil and season with salt and pepper.
- Place the vegetables on the grill or grill pan. Cook, turning occasionally, for about 8-12 minutes, or until the vegetables are tender and have nice grill marks. The cooking time will vary based on the type and thickness of the vegetables.

5. **Prepare the Dipping Sauce (Optional):**
   - While the vegetables are grilling, mix together the soy sauce, rice vinegar, sugar, minced garlic, sesame seeds, green onion, and gochugaru (if using) in a small bowl.
6. **Serve:**
   - Transfer the grilled vegetables to a serving platter.
   - Garnish with chopped green onions and additional sesame seeds if desired.
   - Serve with the dipping sauce on the side, if using.

Tips:

- **Vegetable Variety:** Feel free to use other vegetables such as asparagus, cherry tomatoes, or eggplant. Adjust the grilling time based on the type and size of the vegetables.
- **Marinating:** Marinating adds extra flavor but is optional. For a simpler version, you can skip the marinade and just season the vegetables with salt and pepper before grilling.
- **Grill Pan:** If you don't have a grill, a grill pan or even a broiler can be used to achieve similar results.

Enjoy your Yachae Gui! This grilled vegetable dish is a healthy and flavorful addition to any meal, bringing a touch of Korean cuisine to your table.

Korean BBQ Beef Skewers (Bulgogi)

Ingredients:

- **For the Marinade:**
    - 1/2 cup soy sauce
    - 1/4 cup brown sugar or honey
    - 2 tablespoons sesame oil
    - 2 tablespoons rice wine or mirin
    - 3 cloves garlic, minced
    - 1 tablespoon ginger, minced
    - 1 tablespoon gochugaru (Korean red chili flakes) (optional, for heat)
    - 1 tablespoon sesame seeds
    - 2 green onions, finely chopped
    - 1 pear, grated (or 1/4 cup apple juice as a substitute, for sweetness and tenderizing)
- **For the Beef:**
    - 1 lb (450g) beef sirloin, ribeye, or flank steak, thinly sliced (about 1/4-inch thick)
    - 1 bell pepper, cut into chunks (optional, for skewering)
    - 1 onion, cut into chunks (optional, for skewering)
    - 1 zucchini, cut into chunks (optional, for skewering)
- **For Garnish:**
    - Chopped green onions
    - Sesame seeds

Instructions:

1. **Prepare the Marinade:**
    - In a bowl, mix together soy sauce, brown sugar or honey, sesame oil, rice wine or mirin, minced garlic, minced ginger, gochugaru (if using), sesame seeds, chopped green onions, and grated pear or apple juice.
    - Stir until the sugar is dissolved and all ingredients are well combined.
2. **Marinate the Beef:**
    - Place the thinly sliced beef in a large zip-top bag or shallow dish.
    - Pour the marinade over the beef, ensuring all the slices are coated evenly.
    - Seal the bag or cover the dish and refrigerate for at least 30 minutes to 1 hour. For best results, marinate overnight.
3. **Prepare the Skewers:**
    - If using wooden skewers, soak them in water for at least 30 minutes to prevent burning.
    - Thread the marinated beef slices onto the skewers, alternating with chunks of bell pepper, onion, and zucchini if desired.
4. **Preheat the Grill:**

- Preheat your grill to medium-high heat. If using a grill pan, preheat it over medium-high heat on the stovetop.
5. **Grill the Skewers:**
    - Brush the grill grates or grill pan with a little oil to prevent sticking.
    - Grill the beef skewers for about 2-3 minutes on each side, or until the beef is cooked to your desired level of doneness and has a nice char. Be careful not to overcook the beef, as it can become tough.
6. **Serve:**
    - Transfer the grilled skewers to a serving platter.
    - Garnish with chopped green onions and additional sesame seeds if desired.
    - Serve hot, with a side of steamed rice, kimchi, or a dipping sauce of your choice.

Tips:

- **Beef Choice:** Choose cuts of beef that are tender and flavorful. Flank steak, ribeye, or sirloin are excellent choices.
- **Marinating:** The longer you marinate the beef, the more flavorful and tender it will be. If you're short on time, even a 30-minute marinade will add good flavor.
- **Grilling:** Avoid overcrowding the grill. Grill the skewers in batches if necessary to ensure even cooking and a good char.

Enjoy your Korean BBQ Beef Skewers (Bulgogi)! These savory and sweet skewers are perfect for a summer barbecue or a delicious weeknight dinner.

Spicy Fish Stew (Maeuntang)

Ingredients:

- **For the Stew:**
    - 1 lb (450g) white fish (such as cod, rockfish, or sea bass), cut into chunks
    - 1 tablespoon salt
    - 2 tablespoons vegetable oil
    - 1 medium onion, sliced
    - 1-2 green chilies, sliced (adjust to taste)
    - 2-3 cloves garlic, minced
    - 1 tablespoon ginger, minced
    - 2-3 tablespoons gochujang (Korean red chili paste)
    - 1 tablespoon gochugaru (Korean red chili flakes) (adjust to taste)
    - 2 tablespoons soy sauce
    - 1 tablespoon fish sauce (optional, for extra umami)
    - 6 cups water or fish stock
    - 1 medium potato, peeled and sliced
    - 1 medium carrot, peeled and sliced
    - 1 cup napa cabbage or bok choy, chopped
    - 1-2 green onions, chopped
    - 1 tablespoon sesame oil
    - 1 teaspoon sesame seeds (optional)
- **For Garnish (optional):**
    - Chopped cilantro or parsley
    - Additional sliced green chilies

Instructions:

1. **Prepare the Fish:**
    - Rinse the fish pieces under cold water and pat them dry with paper towels.
    - Sprinkle with salt and let them sit for about 10-15 minutes to season.
2. **Prepare the Stew Base:**
    - Heat vegetable oil in a large pot over medium heat.
    - Add the sliced onion, green chilies, minced garlic, and minced ginger. Sauté for about 2-3 minutes until fragrant and the onions are translucent.
3. **Add the Spices:**
    - Stir in the gochujang (Korean red chili paste) and gochugaru (Korean red chili flakes). Cook for another 1-2 minutes, stirring constantly to blend the flavors.
4. **Add the Liquids:**
    - Pour in the water or fish stock and bring to a boil.
    - Reduce the heat and let it simmer for about 5 minutes to allow the flavors to meld.
5. **Add the Vegetables:**

- Add the sliced potato and carrot to the pot. Simmer for about 10-15 minutes, or until the vegetables are tender.
6. **Add the Fish:**
    - Gently add the fish pieces to the pot. Be careful not to stir too vigorously to avoid breaking up the fish.
    - Simmer for another 5-10 minutes, or until the fish is cooked through and flakes easily.
7. **Finish the Stew:**
    - Stir in the chopped napa cabbage or bok choy. Simmer for an additional 2-3 minutes, or until the greens are wilted.
    - Add the soy sauce and fish sauce (if using). Adjust seasoning to taste with more salt or gochugaru if desired.
8. **Add Final Touches:**
    - Drizzle with sesame oil and sprinkle with sesame seeds if desired.
    - Garnish with chopped green onions and cilantro or parsley if using.
9. **Serve:**
    - Ladle the stew into bowls and serve hot with steamed rice on the side.

Tips:

- **Fish:** Use fresh, firm white fish for the best texture and flavor. Ensure the fish is cut into even pieces for consistent cooking.
- **Spice Level:** Adjust the amount of gochujang and gochugaru based on your preference for spiciness.
- **Broth:** For a richer broth, use fish stock or a mix of water and fish stock.

Enjoy your Maeuntang! This spicy and hearty fish stew is a wonderful representation of Korean comfort food, perfect for warming up and enjoying with family and friends.

Korean Millet Porridge (Gyeolcheon Juk)

Ingredients:

- **For the Porridge:**
    - 1 cup millet
    - 4 cups water or chicken broth
    - 1 tablespoon sesame oil
    - 1-2 tablespoons honey or sugar (adjust to taste)
    - 1/4 teaspoon salt (optional, adjust to taste)
- **Optional Add-ins:**
    - 1/2 cup dried fruits (such as raisins or dates), chopped
    - 1/2 cup nuts (such as almonds or walnuts), chopped
    - Fresh fruits (such as berries or sliced apples)
    - A sprinkle of cinnamon or ground ginger

Instructions:

1. **Rinse the Millet:**
    - Place the millet in a fine mesh strainer and rinse it under cold running water. Rinse until the water runs clear to remove any dust or impurities. Drain well.
2. **Toast the Millet (Optional):**
    - In a large pot, heat sesame oil over medium heat. Add the rinsed millet and toast it for about 2-3 minutes, stirring occasionally, until it becomes fragrant. This step adds a nutty flavor to the porridge.
3. **Cook the Porridge:**
    - Add the water or chicken broth to the pot with the toasted millet. Bring to a boil over high heat.
    - Once boiling, reduce the heat to low and cover the pot. Simmer for about 20-30 minutes, stirring occasionally, until the millet is soft and the mixture has thickened to a porridge-like consistency. If the porridge becomes too thick, you can add a bit more water or broth to reach your desired consistency.
4. **Sweeten and Season:**
    - Stir in honey or sugar, and salt if using. Adjust the sweetness to taste.
5. **Add Optional Ingredients:**
    - If using, stir in chopped dried fruits and nuts during the last 5 minutes of cooking. This will allow them to soften and infuse their flavor into the porridge.
    - You can also add fresh fruits or a sprinkle of cinnamon or ground ginger just before serving for added flavor.
6. **Serve:**
    - Ladle the porridge into bowls. Serve hot, either plain or with your choice of toppings.

Tips:

- **Consistency:** Adjust the consistency of the porridge by adding more liquid if it becomes too thick. Millet absorbs a lot of liquid as it cooks.
- **Nutritional Boost:** For added nutrition, consider incorporating seeds (such as chia or flax seeds) or a spoonful of yogurt as toppings.
- **Flavor Variations:** Experiment with different spices and flavorings, such as vanilla extract or nutmeg, to customize the taste.

Enjoy your Gyeolcheon Juk! This millet porridge is not only a nutritious and comforting meal but also a wonderful way to start your day or enjoy a light, satisfying dish.

Seafood Pancake (Haemul Pajeon)

Ingredients:

- **For the Pancake Batter:**
    - 1 cup all-purpose flour
    - 1/4 cup cornstarch
    - 1/2 teaspoon baking powder
    - 1 cup cold water (adjust as needed for batter consistency)
    - 1 large egg
    - 1/2 teaspoon salt
    - 1/4 teaspoon black pepper
- **For the Filling:**
    - 1/2 cup shrimp, peeled and deveined
    - 1/2 cup squid, cleaned and cut into rings (optional)
    - 1/2 cup mussels or clams (optional, cleaned and pre-cooked)
    - 4-5 green onions, chopped into 1-2 inch pieces
    - 1 small carrot, julienned (optional)
    - 1/2 cup mushrooms, sliced (optional)
- **For Cooking:**
    - Vegetable oil or sesame oil
- **For Dipping Sauce:**
    - 2 tablespoons soy sauce
    - 1 tablespoon rice vinegar or apple cider vinegar
    - 1 teaspoon sugar
    - 1 clove garlic, minced
    - 1 teaspoon sesame seeds
    - 1 green onion, finely chopped
    - 1/2 teaspoon gochugaru (Korean red chili flakes) (optional, for heat)

Instructions:

1. **Prepare the Seafood:**
    - If using frozen seafood, thaw it thoroughly and pat dry with paper towels.
    - Cut the seafood into bite-sized pieces if needed.
2. **Make the Batter:**
    - In a large bowl, mix together the flour, cornstarch, baking powder, salt, and black pepper.
    - Add the cold water and egg, and whisk until smooth. The batter should be thick enough to coat the seafood and vegetables but still pourable. Adjust with more water if needed.
3. **Prepare the Filling:**
    - Gently fold the seafood, green onions, carrot, mushrooms, and any other vegetables into the batter.

4. **Cook the Pancake:**
    - Heat a large skillet or griddle over medium-high heat and add a generous amount of vegetable oil or sesame oil.
    - Once the oil is hot, pour a portion of the batter into the skillet and spread it out into a thin, even layer.
    - Cook for about 3-4 minutes, or until the bottom is golden brown and crispy. Flip carefully and cook the other side for another 3-4 minutes until golden brown and crispy.
    - Repeat with the remaining batter, adding more oil to the skillet as needed.
5. **Make the Dipping Sauce:**
    - In a small bowl, combine soy sauce, rice vinegar, sugar, minced garlic, sesame seeds, chopped green onion, and gochugaru (if using). Stir well to combine.
6. **Serve:**
    - Transfer the cooked pancakes to a cutting board or serving platter. Cut into wedges or squares.
    - Serve hot with the dipping sauce on the side.

Tips:

- **Consistency:** Ensure the batter is not too runny; it should coat the seafood and vegetables well. If it's too thick, add a bit more water.
- **Heat:** Cook the pancakes over medium to medium-high heat to ensure they cook evenly and get crispy without burning.
- **Variation:** Feel free to use different seafood or vegetables based on your preference or what's available.

Enjoy your Haemul Pajeon! This savory seafood pancake is a delightful and flavorful dish that's sure to impress family and friends.

Kimchi and Pork Stir-Fry (Kimchi Jorim)

Ingredients:

- **For the Stir-Fry:**
    - 1 lb (450g) pork belly or pork shoulder, cut into bite-sized pieces
    - 2 cups well-fermented kimchi, chopped into bite-sized pieces
    - 1 tablespoon vegetable oil
    - 1 medium onion, sliced
    - 2-3 cloves garlic, minced
    - 1 tablespoon ginger, minced
    - 1-2 tablespoons gochujang (Korean red chili paste) (optional, for extra spice)
    - 2 tablespoons soy sauce
    - 1 tablespoon sugar (adjust to taste)
    - 1/2 cup water or kimchi juice (from the kimchi jar)
    - 1 tablespoon sesame oil
    - 1 tablespoon sesame seeds (optional, for garnish)
    - 2-3 green onions, chopped (optional, for garnish)

Instructions:

1. **Prepare the Pork:**
    - Heat vegetable oil in a large skillet or wok over medium-high heat.
    - Add the pork pieces and cook until they start to brown and crisp up, about 5-7 minutes.
2. **Add Aromatics:**
    - Add the sliced onion, minced garlic, and minced ginger to the skillet with the pork.
    - Stir-fry for about 2-3 minutes until the onions are translucent and the aromatics are fragrant.
3. **Add Kimchi and Seasonings:**
    - Stir in the chopped kimchi and cook for another 2-3 minutes, allowing the kimchi to release its flavors.
    - If using, add the gochujang (Korean red chili paste) for extra heat and depth of flavor.
    - Stir in soy sauce and sugar, mixing well.
4. **Simmer:**
    - Pour in the water or kimchi juice, and bring to a boil.
    - Reduce the heat to medium-low and let it simmer for about 10-15 minutes, or until the pork is tender and the flavors have melded together. Stir occasionally to prevent sticking.
5. **Finish:**
    - Once the pork is cooked through and the sauce has thickened slightly, stir in the sesame oil for added flavor.
    - Taste and adjust the seasoning with more soy sauce or sugar if needed.

6. **Garnish and Serve:**
    - Transfer the Kimchi Jorim to a serving dish.
    - Garnish with sesame seeds and chopped green onions if desired.
    - Serve hot with steamed rice.

Tips:

- **Kimchi:** Use well-fermented kimchi for the best flavor. If the kimchi is very sour, you might want to balance it with a little extra sugar.
- **Pork:** Pork belly is traditional and adds richness, but pork shoulder or any other cut of pork can also be used if you prefer a leaner option.
- **Spice Level:** Adjust the amount of gochujang and sugar according to your taste preferences. You can also add red pepper flakes for additional heat if desired.

Enjoy your Kimchi Jorim! This dish pairs wonderfully with a bowl of steamed rice and can be complemented with side dishes like pickled radish or steamed vegetables.

Korean Tofu and Vegetable Stir-Fry (Dubujeongol)

Ingredients:

- **For the Stir-Fry:**
    - 1 block (14 oz) firm tofu, drained and cut into bite-sized cubes
    - 1 tablespoon vegetable oil
    - 1 medium onion, sliced
    - 1 bell pepper, sliced (any color)
    - 1 medium carrot, julienned
    - 1 zucchini, sliced
    - 2-3 cloves garlic, minced
    - 1 tablespoon ginger, minced
    - 1-2 tablespoons gochujang (Korean red chili paste) (optional, for extra spice)
    - 2 tablespoons soy sauce
    - 1 tablespoon sesame oil
    - 1 tablespoon sugar (adjust to taste)
    - 1/2 cup water or vegetable broth
    - 1 tablespoon sesame seeds (optional, for garnish)
    - 2-3 green onions, chopped (optional, for garnish)
- **For the Broth (optional but recommended):**
    - 2 cups vegetable broth or water
    - 1 tablespoon soy sauce
    - 1 tablespoon gochujang (Korean red chili paste)
    - 1 teaspoon sugar

Instructions:

1. **Prepare the Tofu:**
    - Drain the tofu and press it gently to remove excess moisture. Cut into bite-sized cubes.
2. **Cook the Tofu:**
    - Heat vegetable oil in a large skillet or wok over medium-high heat.
    - Add the tofu cubes and cook until they are golden brown and slightly crispy on all sides, about 5-7 minutes. Remove the tofu from the skillet and set aside.
3. **Stir-Fry the Vegetables:**
    - In the same skillet, add a little more oil if needed.
    - Add the sliced onion, bell pepper, carrot, and zucchini. Stir-fry for about 3-4 minutes until the vegetables are slightly tender but still crisp.
4. **Add Aromatics:**
    - Add the minced garlic and ginger to the skillet with the vegetables. Stir-fry for another 1-2 minutes until fragrant.
5. **Add Seasonings:**
    - Stir in gochujang (if using), soy sauce, sesame oil, and sugar. Mix well to coat the vegetables evenly.
    - Pour in the water or vegetable broth and bring to a simmer.

6. **Combine Tofu and Vegetables:**
   - Return the browned tofu to the skillet. Stir gently to combine with the vegetables and let it simmer for an additional 5 minutes, allowing the flavors to meld together.
7. **Prepare the Broth (if using):**
   - In a separate pot, combine vegetable broth, soy sauce, gochujang, and sugar. Bring to a simmer and adjust seasoning to taste. Pour over the tofu and vegetables in the skillet, if desired, for a more soupy version of the dish.
8. **Garnish and Serve:**
   - Garnish with sesame seeds and chopped green onions if desired.
   - Serve hot with steamed rice or as a side dish with other Korean meals.

Tips:

- **Tofu:** For a firmer texture, you can use extra-firm tofu. Pressing the tofu before cooking helps remove excess moisture and makes it crispier.
- **Vegetables:** Feel free to use any vegetables you have on hand or your favorites. Common additions include mushrooms or bok choy.
- **Spice Level:** Adjust the amount of gochujang to suit your taste. If you prefer a milder dish, you can omit it entirely or use less.

Enjoy your Dubujeongol! This dish is a flavorful and nutritious way to enjoy tofu and vegetables, and it's versatile enough to adapt to your personal preferences.

Traditional Korean Breakfast (Jangjorim with Rice)

Ingredients:

- **For the Jangjorim:**
    - 1 lb (450g) beef shank or brisket, cut into large chunks
    - 4 cups water
    - 1 tablespoon sesame oil
    - 1 onion, quartered
    - 3-4 cloves garlic, smashed
    - 2-3 dried Korean chilies (optional, for extra flavor)
    - 1/4 cup soy sauce
    - 2 tablespoons sugar (adjust to taste)
    - 1 tablespoon honey or corn syrup
    - 1 tablespoon rice wine or mirin (optional, for extra depth)
    - 4-5 boiled eggs, peeled (optional)
    - 1 tablespoon sesame seeds (for garnish)
    - 2-3 green onions, chopped (for garnish)
- **For Serving:**
    - Steamed white rice

Instructions:

1. **Prepare the Beef:**
    - In a large pot, add the beef chunks and cover with water. Bring to a boil over high heat.
    - Once boiling, remove the beef, discard the water, and rinse the beef under cold water to remove any impurities.
2. **Simmer the Beef:**
    - In the same pot, add 4 cups of fresh water and bring to a boil.
    - Add the cleaned beef chunks, sesame oil, onion, garlic, and dried chilies (if using).
    - Reduce heat to low and simmer, covered, for about 1.5 to 2 hours, or until the beef is tender and easily shredded.
3. **Prepare the Sauce:**
    - Once the beef is tender, remove it from the pot and set aside.
    - In a small bowl, mix together soy sauce, sugar, honey (or corn syrup), and rice wine (if using).
4. **Reduce the Broth:**
    - Increase the heat to medium and let the broth reduce for about 10-15 minutes, until slightly thickened.
5. **Add the Sauce and Beef:**
    - Return the beef to the pot and add the prepared sauce. Stir well to coat the beef evenly.
    - Simmer for an additional 10-15 minutes, allowing the flavors to meld and the sauce to thicken further.

6. **Add Boiled Eggs (Optional):**
   - If using, add the peeled boiled eggs to the pot and gently simmer for another 5-10 minutes, allowing the eggs to absorb some of the flavors.
7. **Garnish:**
   - Sprinkle sesame seeds and chopped green onions over the Jangjorim for garnish.
8. **Serve:**
   - Serve Jangjorim hot with steamed white rice. You can also include some kimchi or other banchan on the side for a complete Korean breakfast.

Tips:

- **Beef:** Beef shank or brisket works best for Jangjorim due to their rich flavor and texture. If using other cuts, ensure they are well-cooked and tender.
- **Sauce:** Adjust the sweetness and saltiness of the sauce to your preference. You can add more sugar or soy sauce if needed.
- **Storage:** Jangjorim can be stored in the refrigerator for several days and often tastes better the next day as the flavors continue to develop.

Enjoy your traditional Korean breakfast of Jangjorim with rice! It's a comforting and flavorful dish that brings together savory, sweet, and slightly spicy elements in a satisfying way.